AUSTERITY AT A GRAVEYARD

Targeting Drivers of Supranational Global Governance

"Commerce cannot be entrusted with the moral interests of mankind. She has no principle that can withstand a strong temptation to her insatiable cupidity."

Joseph Thompson, *The Broken Covenant*, 1857

Contents

I.	Initial Problems with "Prosperity at a Crossroads"	1
II.	"Traded Sectors" & "Drivers" of Economic Growth	7
III.	"Growing" Exports & Declining Productivity	12
IV.	STEM Training	15
V.	Regional Consolidation	17
VI.	Concern for Jobs and Worker Pay	21
VII.	Entrepreneurialism and Its Discontents	23
VIII.	MBA: Assembly Line or Hoax?	27
IX.	Deplorable Science	32
X.	Economics as Pseudo-Science	46
XI.	Rattletraps, Rattlesnakes & Time Bombs	51
XII.	Equality is America's Identity, Not a Brand	57

I. Initial Problems with "Prosperity at a Crossroads"

The June 2014 composition delivered under the auspices of the Brookings Institution, Ewing Marion Kauffman Foundation ("The Foundation of Entrepreneurship"), and Mid-America Regional Council (MARC) raises a number of unregenerate and serious questions, not least of which concern the integrity and motives of its framers. More than twenty pro-business and civic groups have endorsed the report, including the Greater Kansas City Chamber of Commerce, Brookings Metropolitan Policy Program, the Kauffman Foundation and William T. Kemper Foundation, University of Missouri-Kansas City, University of Kansas, Kansas State University, and several think tanks and research groups. With the heavy investment of these boosters in the development outline that their report recommends for Kansas City, Missouri, "Prosperity at a Crossroads: Targeting Drivers of Economic Growth for Greater Kansas City" merits a more discriminating examination than it has received so far. Since the Kauffman Foundation spearheaded production of "Prosperity at a Crossroads," and clearly has the most at stake in its future, I shall refer to this document as the Kauffman Report.

According to its "Preface," this report grew over several years from the "need" of "a number of business, civic and community leaders" for "a more informed discussion" of "the economic future of Greater Kansas City." This is to "help residents and decision-makers...better understand the performance of the region." One would have thought their motive might be employment and job creation. Not surprisingly, they expressed "a desire for sound research and rigorous analysis," also "for more data and resources to better evaluate the kind of policies or strategies that could be pursued..." With a passing nod to the "Great Recession" and "leaner fiscal times," the report "strives" to achieve three overarching goals: "Assess the region's overall economic performance, given today's global, economic and political context," "Conduct focused research in one area of analysis–productivity," and "Suggest a framework for action," especially "implications for further applied research"—surely a curious example of action.

The report hopes to "further the dialogue and collaborations underway...for a stronger community" and "welcomes ideas and ongoing engagement." Since the dialogue and collaborations have

1

already been underway for several years, one can only wonder: engagement with whom? Clearly not with "residents" of Greater Kansas City, already distinguished above as separate from "decision-makers."

This is not simply a matter for the municipality of Kansas City, Missouri or the Midwest. The issues in this report go to the heart of structural problems affecting the whole nation, with implications and consequences that will shape the entire world. The broader deeper issues and our responsibility to confront these challenges with clear thought and direct action are too important for us to let shortsighted interests and sectional or sectarian rivalries blind us to their implications.

"Prosperity at a Crossroads" is not, as it purports to be, an impartial or objective analysis of economic issues relevant to Kansas City, but rather an advertising and propaganda presentation, a kind of "dog-&-pony" show. The Kauffman Report is crafted exclusively from the viewpoint of high-roller investors whose interests it solely represents.

A navy blue ribbon horizontally crosses the cover of the report, bisecting a solid blue image of earth, deliberately obliterating Central America and the upper third of South America, including Ecuador, Columbia, Venezuela, Guyana, Suriname, French Guiana, and approximately 30% of Brazil. Is the geopolitical symbolism deliberate? The blue globe has a glassy reflective quality, like a Christmas tree ornament, a subtle visual suggestion of fragility. The words "Prosperity at a Crossroads" overlay the globe in large, bold, white letters. Light blue continents of North and South America are prominent in the foreground; a bull's-eye targets the heartland, with lines radiating outward from Kansas City to Africa, Europe, Asia, and South America. Carefully positioned off-center and to the right, these images are superimposed against a static background of tight horizontal pinstripes, blue lines against a yellow-green background in the lower third, yellow lines against white dominating the upper two-thirds of the cover.

Ignoring the mostly redundant "Introduction" for the moment, one cannot help noticing that this report is engorged with 33 colorful bar and pie charts, graphs, and graphics, soaking up nearly 16 of the 32

2

pages comprising its text. Well-stocked with footnotes, "Prosperity at a Crossroads" looks impressive. That impression withers upon scrutiny. Of 42 endnotes, 24 cite only "Authors' analysis" (for example "Authors' analysis of Regional Economic Models, Inc. data," "Authors' analysis of Moody's Analytics data," and "Authors' analysis of Census Public Use Microdata"). Four endnotes cite articles produced by the Kauffman Foundation itself, two cite Brookings publications. Since these institutions are also the authors of this report, they are simply citing themselves as authorities in lieu of empirical evidence to support their assertions. Arguments from authority are notoriously unreliable and usually indicate fallacious reasoning. Without offering any evidence or argument, there is simply no proof. Like Bush and Obama administrations, the authors of this report are in effect saying, "We're the experts. Trust us." Mere hand waving should persuade no one.

A June 19, 2014 Kansas City Star editorial warns of a deteriorating economy. The editorial ("Cooperate to inject new life into area economy") based its views on the Kauffman Report. Since both the Star editorial and a report of the local NPR affiliate KCUR-FM[*] raise issues of economic survival, this report merits a thorough and detailed assessment.

"Prosperity at a Crossroads" purports to respond to the internecine Missouri-Kansas "border war," in which each state lures businesses away from the other with lucrative sweetheart deals. The report correctly views this situation as divisive, yet fails to mention that this kind of fierce competition is inherent in the very structure of our existing economic system. That the authors of this report wish to dampen competition is ironical, not to say puzzling, given both the boundless defense of competition as a virtue of "free market" capitalism and the report's subsequent complaint about a "decline in competitiveness."

Brookings senior fellow Amy Liu states that "in the last decade this region is beginning to lag the US" in "job growth, wage growth, and overall economic output growth." MARC director David Warm,

---

[*] "KC CROSSROADS REPORT," Frank Morris, 6/13/14.

observing that changes are necessary, adds that the overall purpose of their report is "to create an alternative narrative to the border war." MARC economist Frank Lenk claims that "five of the six" economic sectors (or "traded clusters") "show some signs of weakness," either "losing market share, or they aren't really adding jobs." How are these claims even distinguishable from the economic effects of the subprime loan scandal and Wall Street Meltdown? Such a reframing of the overall economic downturn smacks of spin, intended to camouflage and distract from the Depression those events triggered, a Depression that, contrary to the Kauffman Report, is certainly ongoing, with social hemorrhaging in millions of foreclosures, unemployed and homeless, and may have begun as early as 2001.

Spokespersons for this report make a great show of a kind of hands-off impartiality in their take on economic issues affecting Greater Kansas City. One wonders whether the very term Greater Kansas City in the report's full title does not actually refer to the Greater Kansas City Chamber of Commerce rather than to the metropolitan area and its inhabitants. Given the Chamber's "Big 5 Initiative" for transforming Kansas City into "America's Most Entrepreneurial City" and its zealous embrace of a Kauffman-esque doctrine of entrepreneurship, it can hardly have been a mere coincidence. "This is not a report that says here's what to do, 1, 2, 3, 4," MARC research director Frank Lenk told KCUR's Frank Morris. "This is a report that says, here's our analysis of the issues. Here's the things we need to be focusing on. Here's some examples of what other folks are doing. Now, Kansas City, what are you going to do?" This gives a nominal impression of not meddling (or invisibility?); however, nothing could be further from the truth. For starters, to depict powerfully positioned organizations like Brookings, Chamber of Commerce, Kauffman, Kemper, and Mid-America Regional Council as "folks" is disingenuous to the point of dissembling; the same sort of blurring of definitional and existential lines that distinguish inanimate corporate organizations from living breathing persons. The report is, in fact, a poison pill intended to frighten citizens into slavishly complying with a predetermined blueprint for advancing the interests of powerful private financial interests.

"Prosperity at a Crossroads" purports to be concerned about declining productivity, jobs and worker pay. What it actually professes is something quite different: it recommends increasing exports and investments in "traded sectors," focusing on STEM training to stimulate innovation, expanding regional consolidation to force cooperation, and reorganizing local municipalities in what the report calls a "Metropolitan Revolution." A careful reading of the report shows that its recommendations entail the opposite consequences for productivity, jobs and worker pay. Without directly saying so, this report is heavily laden with its own mandate and agenda.

There are some initial problems with what the report asserts. Briefly, it maintains that the future of business for Greater Kansas City lies exclusively with our ability to: increase export trade to foreign markets (e.g., China and India), concentrate investment on the "drivers" of productivity and competitiveness ("traded sectors," "traded clusters," "market fundamentals"), redefine education exclusively as STEM training (i.e., training in science, technology, engineering and mathematics), and restructure the region and cities to "align" the states with corporate policy to advance these goals. These, the report implies, will result in maximizing the number of entrepreneurial startups and technological innovations for rapid commercial exploitation (especially the number of patents issued). Let us consider each of these points, one at a time.

We must increase exports to foreign markets for one very simple reason, the report asserts: *Globalization is forcing the U.S. (and the rest of the world) to adapt and transform.* It touts "globalization" and "regions" as "what matters for regional economic growth," as if these were all that mattered. This is true, however, only for industries that require a global transportation infrastructure dependent on fossil fuel. It is far from clear that the need for the U.S. and the world to "adapt and transform" entails the recommendations and aim urged by this report. If, however, we consider an alternative to the kind of "Regional Economic Growth" this report advocates, things appear otherwise. It is unlikely that regional economic growth can be reduced to such a glib pairing; then, too, it raises the issue of *what it is exactly that we want to see grow.*

The economy and society is vibrant with, and poised for, a revolutionary trending away from multinational global domination and toward local self-sufficiency. The only way to be sure that Big Agra and the petrochemical cartels don't wind up poisoning us all in their headlong pursuit of profits is by cultivating local food production systems via small farms, urban rooftop gardens, and self-sufficient, permanent community agriculture (or permaculture) enterprises that utilize aeroponic and hydroponic technologies, minimize the need for nutrients and water (eliminating waste), and integrate their relationship and goals with those of the consumers they serve in their local communities.

Like the "Too Big to Save" banks with which they are entirely complicit, centralized multinational corporations drain all value from local communities to distant repositories of concentrated wealth. Look around at the cities and towns across this nation, the chronically neglected infrastructure, bankrupt schools, increasing number of homeless men, women and children forced to live on the streets, demoralized by 40 years of flat wages, largely the result of corporate monopolies exploiting "efficiencies" resulting from so-called economies of scale. Ask yourself: is Walmart, ExxonMobil and Google likely to get smaller or bigger? A transportation industry and infrastructure designed to ship commodities from one side of the globe to the other is not simply counterintuitive, it is foolish. It makes far more sense for a coffee grower in Kenya to produce and process coffee beans for local consumption than it does to ship raw beans to the U.S. or EU at a price determined by the external market. Just as the local African communities can best nurture and protect the value produced by Kenyan coffee growers, so whatever may be lost in the diminution of cheap products from China, India and Indonesia will be gained everywhere by enhanced food security and by retaining the value citizens create within their local communities. The existing transportation infrastructure serves the U.S. military industrial complex, that is, the corporatized military, not U.S. commerce. Local democratic autonomy offers a much greater capacity to adapt, transform and grow a rational and humane economy that will increase and enhance public happiness than the status quo fare that supranational corporatism promises to serve up.

II. "Traded Sectors" & "Drivers" of Economic Growth

Though I may be pilloried for saying so, the Kauffman Report is evidently confused about exactly what these "drivers" are; for it can't seem to make up its mind what to call them. Like "core curriculum," the Kauffman Report is infatuated with "cores": "core assets," "core issue areas," and "core competencies." The "core drivers of economic growth and prosperity" are *trade, innovation,* and *talent*; these in turn "depend on" *infrastructure, governance* and *social equity*. In an unfortunate but suggestive choice of words, the report calls these last three "enablers" (like enabling an addiction—the addiction to fossil fuel, crisis management and oligarchy).

On the same page, the three italicized "drivers" are suddenly renamed: *"traded clusters"* (a fancy term for cronyism and monopolies, encompassing everything from pool agreements, pledges, escrow deposits, management or service contracts, patent agreements and withholding procedures), *"innovation and entrepreneurship"* (code for technological salvation), while *talent* becomes *"human capital"* (code for money-in-the-form-of-flesh or human trafficking). Among the trio of "enablers," "Governance" (tax and regulatory policies, written by corporate interests) assumes pride of place, while "Infrastructure" (the "built form" of a region oddly includes "physical infrastructure and natural features") is marked by "attractiveness," "environmental health," and most importantly "the ease with which firms, suppliers and workers can connect, improving mobility and productivity." Social Equity now becomes "Social Cohesion and Equity" ("Cohesion" was no doubt added to suggest inclusive equality, a concern supported nowhere else in this report). The hesitation and inability to settle on the name for these all-important drivers of the economy betrays a profound insecurity at the heart of this report.

"Together," the report claims, "these six highly inter-related drivers and enablers produce inclusive prosperity." (Evidently they don't, given what the experts cited so far have to say.) The phrase "inclusive prosperity" is a bit of slick rhetoric to suggest that everyone prospers. Would that include workers? The "fundamental drivers of the economy" are vital, we are told, "because the region's ability to raise standards of living depends on its ability to increase the productivity of its economy—the output per unit of input." The third "driver" (no longer *talent,* now it is "Human Capital") "is the single most important driver of inclusive economic growth," the authors of the report insist. But there is a caveat: "Workers must be able to contribute to and benefit from the regional economy and must have the talent and skills to do so." Attracting and aligning "smart, well-educated" employees must serve "the needs of employers." Corporate hegemony rears its Medusa-like head once again, but because it misconstrues the very purpose of commerce, it gets the relationship backwards. Corporations should serve the needs of consumers and workers, not simply assume that serving the "needs of employers" will automatically do so. Human Capital is talent specially designed to meet specifications laid down by corporate rather than human "need." Such specifications are, as we shall see, inherently arbitrary, subject to change and termination without warning.

Page 31: "More and more regions are turning to the fundamental market drivers of trade, innovation and human capital to drive new sources of growth that will directly benefit firms, workers and communities." Well, not necessarily. The key verbs here are "drive" (and what else would "market drivers" do?) and "will directly benefit." Yet, what or where is the evidence? These particular "market fundamentals" were present on Wall Street, its puppet strings and tentacles snaking throughout the country and the world in 2007, when the greed-run meltdown triggered the Global Depression (it was never a "recession"), a juggernaut from which we have yet to recover.

The Kauffman Report's authors persistently downplay and spin the 2007 Depression. A passing mention of the "wake of the Great Recession" (p. 2), it dissembles with "...the Great Recession has past" (3); and finally "The Great Recession was a wakeup call" (4), all deliberately couched in the past tense to create the desired effect. With millions homeless, foreclosed on, and unemployed, plus a nonexistent "recovery" that mainstream media and even NPR have trouble denying, the Global Depression is not past but passed on (in both senses of the word).

For all the lip service paid to "Social Cohesion and Equity" allegedly enabling "opportunities for all workers and people," there is precious little in this report that doesn't automatically reduce to glib chanting and cheerleading about greater productivity, prosperity, jobs, progress and consumption. "Regions that provide opportunities for all workers and people are more cohesive and prosperous." This is a truism if not a tautology. The implied distinction between "workers and people" here is both odd and ominous. Is it suggesting that the "opportunities" offered to people are different from those to be afforded "workers"? Or that such "opportunities" might involve something other than viable employment at a living wage?

Evidently, the treatment of "drivers" and "enablers" still isn't right, for the report coughs up the notion of "Traded Sectors" on page 15. There are also six of these (the number seems to have a special allure for the authors): Manufacturing, Finance & Insurance, Information, Transportation, Wholesale Trade and Professional Services. One might reasonably ask if these six are not the actual "drivers of economic growth"; but our suspicions are quickly allayed when told that, of these six, only professional services are "firing on all cylinders." Sticking with the ever-popular automotive imagery ("drivers"), "the region's overall economic engine is not fueling high performance." Never mind that no such engine exists, it's another bad metaphor, and high-octane fuel won't help anyone—except (perhaps) ExxonMobil, BP and Chevron.

Only five pages later, the document's designers are forced to ask out of sheer desperation, "What's the difference between a traded sector and traded a [sic] cluster?" This again indicates an inherent unease and uncertainty about supposedly key concepts that is disturbing. Despite the typo, the explanation offered is instructive: "While the classification of individual industries is very detailed, economic data for metropolitan areas is typically reported at the sector level" (sparing the ignorant reader such trivia), "consisting of about 20 broadly defined industries, such as construction," the six traded sectors previously mentioned, "retail trade...and a variety of service industries." Traded sectors, it seems, are responsible for most of a region's exports and imports. Without a shred of evidence to support this claim, we are told that traded sectors "tend to be more innovative than local-serving sectors" because they have to "compete against the rest of the world." Global competition is more likely to spawn frantic crooked dealings than innovation.

9

"Prosperity at a Crossroads" displays a disconcertingly condescending attitude toward the inhabitants of Greater Kansas City and the Region. The authors can't be bothered to define "traded sectors" or clearly distinguish them from "traded clusters" because of the excruciating detail of such definitions and distinctions. This is simply a dodge; the truth is, the authors of this report do not want to distinguish them. It is more than likely that they cannot be meaningfully distinguished.

If the definition of traded sectors is spotty, traded clusters are "a more nuanced concept than a traded sector." This "nuance" dissolves into distinctions of "thin" and "thick" clusters, which reduce to considerations of size and number: not enough large firms defines "thin," "large numbers of companies" denote the "thick" ones (in the latter case, however, only if those "large numbers of companies lead to greater intra-regional competition, *especially for talented workers*." Presumably, the professional services of "headhunters" will be "firing on all cylinders"). Moreover, "thin traded sectors inhibit the flow of people and ideas needed to generate innovation and growth." So, there we have it: Not talent, not "Human Capital," not STEM-training, but more large companies and an increased "flow" of people creates innovation and growth. This fails to reach even the level of operational definition; it is simply a shell game, sleight-of-hand, or worse: sheer word magic. The unjustified and indefensible upshot of this traded cluster of ideas is: Kansas City and the region should focus on high-tech, multinational corporations that can export exclusively to international markets in Asia, the Far East, and Middle East; corporations that constitute "traded clusters," that is, ingrown, convoluted, crony monopolies. Traded, incidentally, doesn't refer to trade or commerce; it means: traded on the stock market, although the report nowhere admits this.

What about small businesses that don't or can't export to China, India and Indonesia: a law office, dental practice, family counseling business, or health clinic? How are they to generate revenue, that is, get paid? "In April 2013, PEGJ[†] launched Seed Chicago, a Kickstarter-based online platform for crowd-funding small businesses across

---

† Chicago's Plan for Economic Growth and Jobs

economically diverse areas." Did you catch that? Non-exporting, local-serving businesses will have to rely on crowd-funding campaigns. This is not so much a plausible strategy for generating income as it is an excuse for crony consultants desiring to foist their "expertise" in social media marketing upon desperate or unwary potential clients. This scheme fits right in with a corporate mentality that eagerly embraces "creative destruction" of small businesses as "progress."

III. "Growing" Exports & Declining Productivity

To survive and thrive economically, the Kauffman Report assures us, we must pour investment dollars into high-tech exports to foreign markets like China, India and Indonesia. "The rise of emerging markets means greater global competition for industries and talent and a shift in global demand to markets outside the United States." What is the proposed solution? Why, "meaningful initiatives to improve growth and prosperity," of course (one hardly wants *meaningless* initiatives). There it is: the foolish notion of Growth as Progress, but the Growth always takes the same ignoble form (mysteriously oblivious to public need or good), and the "Progress" is always just out of reach.

"The region has an opportunity to take those efforts to *the next level*" (my italics, indicating gamers' jargon). Kansas City must increase its exports, this report urges, hawking "a vision in which the nation and its regions export more, innovate in what matters, and ensure the economy brings people forward rather than leaving them behind." Yet it is anything but clear just how exporting "more" is going to accomplish either the goal of innovation or a fair and inclusive distribution of prosperity implied by the euphemistic phrase "brings people forward." What it declares, though surreptitiously, is a wholehearted commitment to Social Darwinism, an economic "survival of the fittest" in which the growing number of "losers" grows poorer while the minority of "winners" gets ever more deeply entrenched in concentrated wealth and power.

Global trade "between countries more than tripled, from $6.8 trillion to $21.5 trillion" (the footnote accompanying this fabulous claim cites only "Authors' analysis of World Trade Organization Statistics"). Ironically, this trade growth figure of $21.5 trillion closely matches the (lower) estimate James S. Henry cites for missing global wealth and lost taxes in the study, "The Price of Offshore Revisited."[‡]

By its own account, "Prosperity at a Crossroads" focuses on only one area of analysis: productivity. According to the Kauffman Report's

---

[‡] NEW ESTIMATES FOR "MISSING" GLOBAL PRIVATE WEALTH, INCOME, INEQUALITY, AND LOST TAXES, Tax Justice Network, July 2012.

view of things, productivity and competitiveness in Kansas City are declining. The reason? We have lost our "productivity advantage."

What exactly is a "productivity advantage"? Despite its alleged concern for flagging productivity and competitiveness, the Kauffman Report's entire account of productivity is incoherent and indefensible. "What do we mean by output and productivity?" its authors have to ask:

> "Output is an estimate of the total net value produced by business establishments in the Greater Kansas City region. It is a net figure because it subtracts the cost of inputs by area businesses from the value of what they sell."

However, this is a skewed notion of productivity defined only in the aggregate ("total net value"), not productivity in which profits are equitably distributed across the population, so it is misleading. Who cares if U.S. GDP quadruples, when jobs are bled by the millions, quality of life takes a nose-dive, and cities are thrown into receivership to be managed by corporate lawyers and bankers that preempt local autonomy?

Try again.

> "Productivity is a measure of how well businesses are able to create value by transforming inputs into more useful outputs. While the economy grows when firms add more workers, those workers' standard of living can grow only if the firms become more productive, producing more output per worker over time."

Again: without considering how the profits from that productivity are distributed, those standards of living will not grow. Kauffman's purported definition is sheer nonsense. The following sentence of the report tells you why.

> "Moreover, there is often little reason for firms to add workers unless they out-compete rivals by producing better goods and services for less cost."

American English doesn't get much vaguer or more vacuous than the phrase "create value." Benoit Mandelbrot writes that "there are no good valuation formulae." [See Benoit B. Mandelbrot and Richard L.

13

Hudson, *The (mis)Behavior of Markets: A Fractal View of Risk, Ruin, and Reward*, New York: Basic Books/Perseus Books Group, 2004, p. 271.] To suggest that one can create value "by transforming inputs into more useful outputs" is semantic chicanery, the kind of expedient utilitarian gibberish only a Donald Rumsfeld could love. This is like explaining why a sleeping pill works by claiming that it has a sleep-inducing property (no doubt the intended effect of "Prosperity at a Crossroads"). Cost-efficiencies actually force the production of ever-shoddier goods that will sooner need replacing and so accelerate or at least perpetuate the consumption needed to keep currencies (i.e., profits) flowing. The very idea that you can increase wages, improve worker standards of living, or enhance the quality of life across communities by simply flogging productivity (and consumption!) into ever-greater levels of performance is specious, like whipping a slave to make him work harder. Productivity in the United States has increased dramatically and profits soared for decades, yet wages have remained stagnant since the 1970s.

IV. STEM Training

"Greater Kansas City has a skilled workforce, but is not educating and retaining enough workers to meet future demand. ...The region has not produced enough STEM-qualified workers to keep pace with employers' demand and its ability to attract talent from elsewhere has diminished."

"Prosperity at a Crossroads" repeatedly urges us to replace general education with STEM training, that is, training in science, technology, engineering and mathematics. We're just not producing enough educated workers to keep pace with employer demand. More STEM training is the answer to our prayers, by Gates! The need is rather for "replacing retiring workers and educating and training a more diverse replacement workforce," trends that are "playing out inside workforce and education systems." They certainly are and the stress is clearly on *replacement*.

Why not replace all education with STEM training while we're at it? We'll reserve genuine education—advanced degrees in liberal arts and sciences—for the corporate aristocrats of the 1% and their heirs. Minorities, a shredded middle class, the working poor, the destitute and disabled, we'll simply shunt them off to failing schools, siphoning those few we can salvage into STEM programs, while confining the rest to a future glut of highly mobile, desperate, and pliable workers. Or soldiers. By eliminating Social Security, Medicare and the rest of entitlements, we can force everyone into accepting a constricted labor market to supply cheap labor, and force the unwashed majority to work for subsistence.

There it is: the multinational agenda of corporate capitalist hegemony.

By replacing traditional public education with privatized STEM training, multinational corporations will effectively control the future of education. They claim this will improve education, but the last thing they want is an educated citizenry that could call into question the authority and practices of a corporate-controlled government or corporate global governance. The strategy aims really to provide private testing and management companies with new sources of revenue. By controlling the university and college funding, they will also control research outcomes.

15

Focusing education at every level on STEM disciplines, the Kauffman Report insists, will stimulate innovation for quick commercial monetization.

Whenever an official was charged with corruption in ancient Rome, the people asked but a single question: *Qui bono? Who benefits?* In whose interest is it to proclaim a dramatic decline in productivity or an insufficiently educated work force?

V. Regional Consolidation

Regions have a new role to play, according to the creators of this report, but you'd be hard pressed to figure out exactly what that role is on page 6 where it introduces the subject. "Entitlements and interest payments are crowding out federal discretionary spending in economic development priorities such as trade and smarter investments in innovation, infrastructure and education." In case you missed it, the gist here is that citizens tax dollars ("federal discretionary spending") ought to subsidize "investments in innovation, infrastructure and education." No mention of corporate business paying for anything. Well, that *is* a "smarter investment."

With that, the Kauffman Report drops all talk of regional development. We are on the threshold of a "Metropolitan Revolution," the report now reveals. Cities are to be the focus. Why? That's where the population growth is, silly. People in China and India aren't moving to rural farms and villages out in the boonies, they're moving to Beijing and Shanghai and Mumbai. Besides, under the bidding of ALEC, mega-billionaires like the Koch brothers, Pete Peterson, Sheldon Adelson and other closet fascists, big business has done about all the damage it can to Washington, DC and state capitals across the country.

"The Great Recession was a wakeup call." It most certainly was. But according to page 4 of the Kauffman Report, the problem was that "most regions did not respond quickly enough." Not human agency, nor the immoral, predatory and criminal actions of bankers, investors and the top tier of executive management in the financial industry but rather it was "regions" which forced bankruptcy, unemployment and homelessness on millions. The idea is too farcical to merit further scrutiny, let alone refutation.

The ultimate goal is to consolidate the region. This will require taking control of metropolitan areas and forcing them to "focus on market fundamentals." In case we had forgotten, those are the "fundamental market drivers of trade, innovation and human capital to drive new sources of growth that will directly benefit firms, workers and communities." But, to be blunt, the report doesn't really mean it. For any "alternative" to doing what this report recommends will result in "a stagnant region, or worse, a declining one that's much harder to resuscitate in the future." The ultimate goal is to consolidate and plunder the region.

The fanatic need to increase and accelerate the rate of consumption is the sole rationale for gutting the federal bureaucracy, eroding the tax base, privatizing the Post Office, Social Security and Medicare, and perhaps most importantly, maintaining the status quo, power and privilege enjoyed by fossil fuel, nuclear power, pharmaceutical, the Pentagon-driven permanent war economy, finance and insurance. By so doing, the Petrochemical State destroys any possibility of being regulated and expropriates all financial benefit at the cost of the well-being of citizens, youths and seniors alike, forcing them along with all salaried workers to seek jobs at lower pay for longer hours. That is the reason behind the need to control cities, regions and states proposed in this report. These lucrative enterprises, by the way, all but guarantee the continued flourishing of the drug cartels and inevitable wars on drugs and terror, prostitution and child pornography. Profits and the maximizing of profits: isn't that the purpose of capitalism?

"Truly *transformative investments*, by contrast, aim to build *next-economy* sectors within regions that help firms and workers flourish and *enhance global competitiveness*" (more euphemistic jargon). Oh, really? And how might they do that? That reference to "next-economy" is Paul Hawken-talk. Hawken wrote a popular book called *The Next Economy* in 1983 and co-authored *Natural Capitalism: Creating the Next Industrial Revolution* with Amory and Hunter Lovins in 1999. Activist and social entrepreneur, Hawken has recently given talks on "regeneration" and the "meaning of wild" at a conference of the Bioneers, a non-profit organization promoting entrepreneurial environmental activism clothed in the edifying garb of New Age spirituality. Without wishing to impugn the motives of Hawken, the Lovinses, or Bioneers, I merely observe that such talk, which amounts to proselytizing on behalf of an imminent "new world" of happy campers living in perfect harmony with the natural world, inadvertently serves the purposes of the supranational corporate hegemony that is actually running the show. These "masters of war" want a "new world" too and are superhumanly adept at adjusting their double-speak to suit the needs of all such self-maximizing preference seekers.

> Metropolitan areas like Greater Kansas City concentrate the nation's economic assets. The 100 largest metropolitan areas account for two-thirds of U.S. population, three-fourths of jobs and four-fifths of economic output. They produce 72 percent of international service exports, 92 percent of patents and house 74 percent of the college educated ("Prosperity at a Crossroads," page 6).

With their gutted tax base, eroded infrastructure, and spiraling costs, cities across America not surprisingly are proving easy targets for executive management to work with (or, more accurately, co-opt); easier to manipulate than statehouses, and much easier than the federal government. "...city led innovation is paving the way for continued prosperity in our nation. City leaders are the ones reshaping our economy and forging a bipartisan path forward." That ought to succor (or sucker?) every mayor, city council, governor and state house in the land. Nothing like buttering up elected officials to get the juice flowing. So, start with the cities, consolidate the regions under the corporate flag of entrepreneurship, expanding outward until, like Sherwin Williams, you "Cover the Earth." This is the historic pattern of multinational corporate exploitation in the grand tradition of the Dutch and British East Indies Companies. Just as Big Agra in Malawi and India are confiscating the land and livelihood of subsistence farmers in order to convert agriculture to cash crops like tobacco and sugar for export, so large corporate interests in the U.S. are dismantling the middle class, organized labor and the poor. This does not constitute progress, but its opposite.

To recap the "story" that the Kauffman Report wishes to sell: Globalization is forcing the U.S. (and the rest of the world) to adapt and transform. Productivity and competitiveness in Kansas City are declining; we have lost our "productivity advantage." To survive and thrive economically, we must pour investment dollars into high-tech exports to foreign markets like China, India and Indonesia, focus education at every level on STEM disciplines (science, technology, engineering and math) to stimulate innovation that can be quickly capitalized commercially, and restructure our cities, town and regions.

The point is obvious: there is really no alternative to following the plan outlined in this report. After all, we don't want to wind up like Detroit, do we? If that sounds like a threat, it is; and the threat is plain: unemployment, foreclosure, blight and homelessness.

For 17th century Puritans in America, confusion and ruin were infallible signs of innate depravity. Being unemployed under capitalism in modern America is the equivalent of excommunication, of damnation, of not having a soul in the Middle Ages. See how far we've come? Under the gun of such dire exigencies, we entirely overlook the important questions, the ones we should be asking. What are jobs for? What is the purpose of employment and work?

The most despicable thing about "Prosperity at a Crossroads" is the way it pretends to offer a path to economic recovery for all citizens while carefully disavowing any responsibility for whatever actually happens, the ultimate denouement. The report is thus an insurance policy to protect its owners from backlash and blowback, who can chide the communities they fail with "*Tsk, tsk.* Told you so." *We gave you the models, the plan, the tools. You didn't follow through, Kansas City.*

It is unlikely, however, that the proposals in the Kauffman Report will produce jobs for a majority of citizens, even if scrupulously implemented. On the report's own account of matters, the region is not producing enough STEM-trained workers to meet employers' demand and the meticulously documented "educational achievement gaps" among blacks and Hispanics lead inescapably to higher income inequality. The worrisome trends include such warnings as "local demand for educated workers is exceeding supply" and "Greater Kansas City's ability to attract talent has declined." In addition, the report anticipates that automation will replace nearly half (47%) of all U.S. jobs by mid-century. In effect it predicts "a stagnant region, or worse, a declining one that's much harder to resuscitate in the future." Better watch out, Greater Kansas City. *You've been warned.*

VI. Concern for Jobs and Worker Pay

While "Prosperity at a Crossroads" affects concern for wages and workers, it is only lip service paid on one or two occasions. The report offers no serious proposals for implementing wage increases for workers. "For a region to be prosperous," it pontificates, "it must be able to generate wealth that can lead to more jobs and better incomes for workers and firms." Here we have the same old tired values of competition, growth, more and better progress defining consumption-driven capitalism. Here is the crux of the report's argument:

> Since the 1990s, the Greater Kansas City region has generally kept pace with the nation on economic output, employment and wages, with all three performing only slightly below the national average. However, these trends are not translating into improved productivity and living standards for residents.

And why not? Reasons that come readily to mind include: structural inequality, unfair distribution, 44 years of wage stagnation, and the 1% rip-off serving the vested interests of multinational corporations. But not according to Kauffman, Kemper, Brookings and MARC; rather, the region's "productivity advantage" has declined. Or no, not even declined; it's "been eliminated when measured by output per dollar spent on labor compensation" (pp. 2, 10). *If only they didn't have to pay workers!* These authors have confused their own spurious jargon ("productivity advantage") with a reality much closer to home. What they really mean is "profits" interpreted as shareholder profits and executive bonuses.

The "real wages of Greater Kansas City's workers are not keeping up with the nation, with the bottom 70 percent experiencing steeper declines and the top 30 percent experiencing smaller increases." What do you expect? Pushing "right to work (for less)" legislation, eradicating taxes, undermining public education and single-payer healthcare (the preferred choice of the vast majority of Americans, according to every reliable poll), eliminating pensions, breaking unions, firing teachers and threatening to fire public and private sector workers are among the causal forces responsible for these deficits. Increasing consumption and forcing everyone to become an "entrepreneur"—fat chance, that—is not going to affect these trends,

21

but will only postpone the inevitable, namely: the replacement of labor by automation and the elimination of most jobs.

In yet another feeble show of empathy, "Prosperity at a Crossroads" reports that workers may "benefit from the regional economy" but only if they "have the talent and skills to do so." All blame is attributable to individuals, who, if they fail, obviously lack the talent and skills necessary to succeed. Attracting and aligning "smart, well-educated" employees must serve "the needs of employers." Thus, the corporate system invests its Social Darwinism with an air of inevitability, a brutal dynamic that does nothing to shield individuals, ordinary citizens, and their families from ultimate demise.

VII. Entrepreneurialism and Its Discontents

A closer look at the cluster of notions constituting entrepreneurial capitalism is long overdue. Supranational capitalism incorporates an ideology that consists of the following seven beliefs: expansive free will, boundless optimism about the future, exceptionalism, technological salvation, the necessity of working for money, the intrinsic dignity of all such work, and unlimited progress. Because I have analyzed these at length elsewhere[§], I shall limit myself to a brief summary of the argument.

All seven beliefs are demonstrably false. Expansive free will is simply the idea that "Whatever a man wills, he can do" (Hugo Gernsback). The belief that individuals possess a "self-determining power in the will" that gives them carte-blanch freedom to choose right or wrong, good or evil is not only incoherent, it is inconsistent and unempirical. Jonathan Edwards, America's first philosopher, demolished this belief in the 18th century. Historian Perry Miller explained Edwards' position by observing that "no man can be any freer than to be able to do what he wills." As Miller explains: "The notion that a man can cause whatever results he happens to prefer was not only bad theology, it was perverted physics." In his 1949 biography of Edwards, Miller summarizes Edwards' position in this way (calling it "not quite a vulgarization"): "you are free to do what you can do, but you are not free to do what you won't do. You are prevented by walls or by congenital idiocy..." Rejecting their historic beliefs in God's sovereignty and sheer human limitation in favor of a covenant theory whereby man bargains with God to extort salvation, New England businessmen embraced the idea of an expansive free-will because it was more conducive to their prospects in an expanding 18th century economy. Buried within Calvinism, however, lay the germ of another idea, a notion of man's special status: "that man acts outside the field of cause and effect," that he is above the natural order, "that he is a self-originating power." Properly denominated as pride, arrogance and hubris, an equating of man and God, this notion fed the ideology of entrepreneurial capitalism in the 18th century and continues to do so

---

[§] *Sinister Dynamic: Global Governance and the Reconstruction of Nature,* Volume One, *The Axis of History*, October Surprise, 2014, pp. 120-129, 130-133.

today; it is the denial of any distinction between human fabrication and the natural universe. This ultimately is the explanation for modern supranational capitalism's program and agenda: *the Reconstruction of Nature* in its own corporate image.

Once this particular construction of free will is undermined, the subsidiary notions of boundless optimism about the future, exceptionalism, technological salvation, unlimited progress, and work all dissolve. In the Christian context, the need to work is supposedly God's punishment for Adam's original sin, telling wayward mankind in effect:

> *...cursed is the ground because of you; in toil you shall eat of it all the days of your life. Thorns and thistles it shall bring forth to you; and you shall eat the plants of the field. In the sweat of your face you shall eat bread till you return to the ground, for out of it you were taken. You are dust, and to dust you shall return. (Genesis, 3:17-20)*

No CEO ever delivered so devastating a plant closing announcement to shocked employees! Such a view is not unique to Protestantism, but permeates every denomination and branch of institutional Christianity. Expansive free will (we might also term human willfulness, intransigence, and egotism) certainly helps prop up belief in the necessity and intrinsic dignity of work, although it might well be seen as the efficient cause of original sin. Eve, you may recall, got it worse than Adam:

> *To the woman he said, "I will greatly multiply your pain in childbearing. In pain you shall bring forth children, yet your desire shall be for your husband, and he shall rule over you."*

Apparently, Jehovah was no fan of organized labor and collective bargaining or feminism and equal rights (no surprise where western Judeo-Christian patriarchy got its role model). Despite the imputed theological justification, the necessity of work is nothing more than the idea that one has to earn money to live. The Deity's authorization is mere window dressing.

While work, in the sense of meaningful activity, is vital for humans, working for money to "earn one's living" is not. Surely, one has

24

earned one's living by virtue of having survived the vicissitudes of birth, infancy, childhood and adolescence to attain something resembling responsible adulthood. A well-ordered state will do a better job on behalf of all its citizens by eliminating the obstacles to implementing collective ideals of democracy, equality, compassion and social justice rather than condoning or buttressing the solipsistic individualism of a Rumsfeld, a Cheney, or a Bush.

The imputation of intrinsic dignity is the idea that work possesses intrinsic dignity equivalent to and coterminous with human dignity. Dignity or moral worth is a property of all living beings (including human beings). Work and labor as such possess no intrinsic dignity or moral worth. This, along with the idea that there is some moral duty to work, is a myth of the oligarchy or ruling class, originally imposed to keep the masses occupied, maintain productivity and wealth flowing upward to the oligarchs, whether they are landed gentry or Wall Street "banksters." Bertrand Russell's observation is as apt today as it was in 1935: "Modern methods of production have given us the possibility of ease and security for all; we have chosen, instead, to have overwork for some and starvation for others." As Russell stated with compact clarity: "The morality of work is the morality of slaves; and the modern world has no need of slavery." Capitalism, unfortunately, does require slavery; hence the explosion of organized crime in the form of trafficking in humans, weapons and illegal drugs, internet pornography, child abduction and prostitution.

These seven premises are the chief ingredients of entrepreneurship, the ideological justification for modern capitalism and the monetary-market system for which it stands. Accepting them as true makes American exceptionalism—the belief that history or God has uniquely chosen America to rule the world—look obvious. Understanding why they are false renders exceptionalism untenable—not just for America but, mutatis mutandis, for any nation. All seven ingredients and the corporate entrepreneurial ideology that subsumes them are driven by profit-maximization. To state entrepreneurial capitalism's ideological substance succinctly: Success in business can be taught (and thus learned) by everyone and is largely a matter of applying relevant knowledge, marketing skills, a positive attitude, and hard work to discover or create opportunities to exploit new markets (unmet needs).

In other words: *I have free will so I can work hard to acquire dignity and money by succeeding in business as an entrepreneur who innovates new technological improvements that will advance the cause of human progress and justify our boundless optimism about the future, thereby vindicating the doctrine of American exceptionalism.* That is a patent absurdity. To quote philosopher John McMurtry from Peter Joseph's documentary film, *Zeitgeist: Moving Forward*:

> This system is more wasteful than all the other existing systems in the history of the planet. Every level of life organization and life system is in a state of crisis and challenge and decay or collapse. No peer-reviewed journal in the last 30 years will tell you anything different: that is, that every life system is in decline as well as social programs, as well as our water access. Try to name any means of life that isn't threatened and endangered. You can't. There really isn't one and that's very, very despairing. But we haven't even figured out the causal mechanism. We don't want to face the causal mechanism. We just want to go on. You know, that's where insanity is, where you keep doing the same thing over and over again even though it clearly doesn't work. So, you're really dealing with not an economic system but I would go so far as to say an anti-economic system.

And, if the utilitarian principle of "the greatest happiness of the greatest number (of people)" is to be our standard for measuring, then wherever in the world we look, whether the U.S., Europe, Middle East, Africa, Asia, or India, the majority of people are not very happy. And we can't all move to Denmark.

VIII. MBA: Assembly Line or Hoax?

An unpaginated advertising supplement to a July 13-August 10, 2014 publication of the Kansas City Star Media Company, *MBA & Education* reveals the ideological fault lines of corporate capitalism. "Advance your career," K-State University advises, while KU simply proclaims, like gangster Johnny Rocko in *Key Largo*: "I want more." Friends University offers "Education for a better life," while Jesuit Rockhurst University's program, underwritten by Helzberg Jewelry, explains "why it's not just an MBA" ("It's a Helzberg MBA"). Webster University invites prospective students to "Be the next Difference Maker"; Missouri Western specifies several benefits, including "Career advancement," "Job security" and "Higher income" while Park University shouts that "SERIOUS FUN" is the proper adjective to describe "taking your career to the next level."

Baker University sells "momentum…in today's competitive business environment," unintentionally suggesting (perhaps) that the race is not always to the swift. Not only can Washington University's Olin Business School teach you to "Think Like A Leader," it will make you one. Could we expect any less from "the top-ranked local MBA" ("ranked #12 by *U.S. News and World Report*")? UMKC's Henry Bloch School of Management pings carefully chosen notes of "Civic Engagement" and "Innovative Mindset" alongside its other two program "platforms" ("Global Perspective" and "Leadership"), while cagily inserting mantra-like boasts to take "career success to the next level" and prepare "leaders like you…for the next challenge." No doubt distinguishing itself from its St. Louis rival, the Bloch ad simply defines *its* Executive MBA: "Where Innovation Leads." Whether this says something about innovation or merely cites itself as destination, the ambiguous slogan is silent.

A prominent headline emphasizes "joint partnerships" for "today's MBA programs," like UMKC's links "with many schools throughout China." Local Kansas City companies like Cerner, Garmin and Burns & McDonnell (these "major KC employers" are "the heart of our employment base") "are all multinational companies." More importantly, according to this advert, these big multinational players are models for "smaller firms," citing the case of a "small KC company that sells decorative pillows with materials made from

Africa, manufactured in Asia for sale in the U.S." The idea is of course to "broaden" hearts and minds: that is, to replace a student's "Midwestern mindset" with the "global mindset" that multinational corporations prefer.

Other truths slip out between the lines of this blatantly self-serving ad-copy. Under the theme of *Universities offer career support for graduating students*, the Executive MBA program at Washington University's Olin Business School in St. Louis boasts that it offers its students the "personal, confidential, and in-depth" consulting services of an "executive career coach." But, despite these "perks," the anonymous copy is careful to remind its target audience that it is only those MBA graduate students who are "able to effectively use" their acquired skills "in various settings" that will "clearly benefit" from the degree. Lest all the clamoring inducements close the sale for spellbound or gullible provincials, the copy covertly adds the fine print: "no degree has a guarantee of employment."

"Big data and analytics are definitely here to stay," insists Bloch School MBA program director Roger Alan Pick under its banner: *MBA education incorporating social media, big data, analytics*. The program directors square off like linemen to trumpet this message. Helzberg School's program director Myles Gartland thinks "big data and analytics" are "two sides of the same coin" (a favorite analogy among proselytizers on behalf of entrepreneurial science), stressing that coin's importance by noting that Rockhurst has created "two new MBA concentrations and graduate certificate" to make sure graduates are "comfortable" plowing those two immense fields.

Executive director for UMKC's Executive MBA program Kimberly Young reiterates the notion that big data and analytics are here to stay. Though nowhere defining what "big data" and "analytics" are (possibly one reason they are "here to stay"), one rightly infers that these honorific god-words denote nothing more than massive data collection (familiar in another context, namely, Edward Snowden's revelations about the NSA and private sector) in the hope of detecting useful empirical generalizations.

Still more troubling is Young's blithe assertion that the mere "capacity to collect data" itself constitutes knowledge of "inherent opportunities"—and here is where the assumed "science" dissipates in convoluted mists of marketing hype—"to *help* our client organizations and students serve customers better and *help* them to explore untapped market opportunities by *helping* them to better understand where to find data in their organization and then how to analyze the data meaningfully." To which the only appropriate response is: "*Help!*" Curious how the "data" that will help them to explore untapped market opportunities presumably lies not in the world but "in their organization" (does this ambiguous term, "organization," refer to those aforementioned "client organizations" or to some personal power of arranging data?). Realizing that *untapped market opportunities* means only *unrecognized and so unmet needs* (whether genuine or merely fabricated), the ad hoc phrase "how to analyze the data meaningfully" further complicates the puzzle by begging the question as to the very integrity of its supposed "science." The inescapable implication is that "big data" is not being used to detect empirically valid generalizations but rather to endorse marketing strategies and ad-copy supported by convenient but spurious data correlations designed to manipulate mass behavior and promote consumption.

Debbie Psihountas, Webster's MBA director, says big data is a focus for her faculty. "We have new certificate options to allow students to build skills in these areas. The proliferation of data…is increasing and more and more, the challenge isn't getting information, it is how to use it in a meaningful way." One rightly suspects that the only criterion of meaningfulness here is the bluntly utilitarian one of expediting instrumental means to approved ends.

Finally, *Local businesses key in incorporation of innovation in MBA programs* confronts us with a dilemma: are we talking about genuine innovation or only steeping student mindsets in, and inoculating future employees with, incestuous propaganda jargon and hype? There are "new and innovative things" that "various programs" are "implementing," an "integral part in preparing today's students to be tomorrow's businesses leaders." If this sounds like an Army recruitment campaign, that is precisely what it is. Roger Alan Pick says "the role of innovation is huge" (no doubt influenced by the "big data"). Webster's program reviews its course offerings to ensure they are still "on the cutting edge of innovation." Kimberly Young states unequivocally "innovation is about the future." But, if innovation is about the future, how huge can it be? The same impartial experts are dutifully quoted, each with his own turf to defend. Helping is huge for the entrepreneurial missionary zeal: Psihountas cites how they've "helped businesses" by offering "our MBA credential...on site" to client organizations' employees enrolled in their program.

What all this really amounts to, Young astonishingly admits, is "looking at trends to place bets on the future of the Executive MBA program." That, I may remark, is the definition of self-serving. Told that these administrators "speak the language" of their client organizations "around succession planning and talent management" (what language is that?), Young adds: "This is ground breaking in the academic environment." Actually, it is anything but. Colleges and universities have always been concerned at all levels with hiring and promotion (the meaning of Young's euphemistic "succession planning and talent management"); it's just that the criteria for these activities have changed, been reduced exclusively to those of entrepreneurial, multinational, corporate culture.

Conversations with local businesses led directly to Rockhurst's "data science programs," says Helzberg School of Management Dean Cheryl McConnell. "Companies...needed people with that skill set" but they could not find them. Talk about untapped market opportunities! Helping is mutual, for the "cohorts" (i.e., the companies) have proved instrumental, McConnell claims, in helping Rockhurst design its curriculum each year with "what businesses need and expect from MBA graduates." But if, as Olin's assistant dean Meg Shuff insists, "Innovation is the heart of their Executive MBA program," is "an evolving curriculum" intended to "meet the needs of executive students, large corporations and entrepreneurs" or simply achieve "the delivery of the program" itself? If the category of "executive student" strikes one as a pandering oxymoron, how is it that "nothing can replace the live classroom experience and the power of the cohort that our Executive MBA offers?" Does this "evolving curriculum" offer a genuine education or ideological indoctrination plus potential job placement for a select minority instead? If these programs are so dependent on input from cohort client businesses for the "evolving" content of their curriculum, they aren't really educating anyone but are merely providing a specialized set of advertising, employment and PR-management services to an evolving market of captive commercial and investment audiences, most of which are bound to fail.

MBA & Education was part of a larger tabloid, *ARTSKC at Work*: in what has become an increasingly popular PR move for multinational corporations, companies like Black & Veatch, Garmin, Kansas City Power & Light, and Sprint sponsor local artists in, for example, visual arts, cinema, music and dance. With flatulent japes like "Home is Where the Art Is," "Vote for Art!" and "Most Artistic Company Award," the whole project is intended to marshal the arts in the service of corporate business. *ARTSKC at Work* is at best interested in commercially profitable art, that is, art with investment potential. Coolly declaring, "art and work are not separate, but intertwined," it deliberately conflates the two. Lest anyone accuse Star Media or ARTSKC of a disinterested commitment to the arts, the entire pageant serves to showcase its multinational corporate sponsors, for it is the "artistic talents of their employees" that are exclusively spotlighted.

DST's profile is perhaps most intriguing, for it "delivers industry experience, technological expertise and service excellence to help our clients process, communicate and safeguard the critical, high-value information their customers need to manage life's most important business." Without explicitly stating what that "most important business" might be, one hardly knows whether DST is a front for the NSA or a designer of financial software for a diverse set of business applications (apparently its actual business). –Maybe it is both. Among other things, DST's website makes the following boast to potential clients: *"Take advantage of today's challenges by seamlessly connecting customer information to growth strategies."*

IX. Deplorable Science

The "social science" of economics that allegedly supports most of the contentions in "Prosperity at a Crossroads" is deplorable, not really science at all, but rather pseudo-science, as an examination of four key papers cited in the Kauffman report confirms.

The burden of *The Hidden STEM Economy* [Jonathan Rothwell, Brookings Metropolitan Policy Program, 2013] is to enlarge and promote investment in admittedly expensive STEM training, thereby implying that STEM training will be a job-creator. "Some may assume the concept of STEM is a fleeting fad for policymakers, but there are compelling reasons to believe that STEM-related employment is a fundamental aspect of modern economies and that the prominence of STEM jobs will continue to grow as nations industrialize their way to higher standards of living and more complex forms of production and exchange" (pp. 5-6). It is hard to tell exactly what those "compelling reasons" might be. The ones indicated (lots of jobs do require STEM knowledge, STEM jobs available to those lacking four-year degrees are more widely distributed across metropolitan areas, and "sub-bachelor's level training" is underfunded) are as dependent on assumption as the claim that greater industrialization leads either to "higher standards of living" or "more complex forms of production and exchange." The conclusion that half of all STEM jobs are available to those without a four-year college degree (p. 1) would seem to undermine the alleged importance of STEM training altogether.

Tech Starts: High-Technology Business Formation and Job Creation in the United States was published in August 2013 as part of the Kauffman Foundation Research Series: Firm Formation and Economic Growth. The fact that its author "Ian Hathaway is an economic advisor to Engine, a research foundation and policy coalition for technology startups" would seem to pose a conflict of interest.

"Few new businesses will ever grow substantially or innovate," Hathaway acknowledges on page 3. Yet, as the paper's title implies: "...new and young firms in this sector play an especially outsized role in net job creation." —This is what the paper assumes and then goes on to conclude. But where is the proof? All of these papers do a lot of hand waving about the vibrancy of entrepreneurship, as we shall see, yet Hathaway admits that his own research may reflect "...an underlying decline in business dynamism and entrepreneurship" (p. 8).

"The presence of entrepreneurship in a region has been consistently linked with measures of economic development, such as employment growth," Hathaway asserts (p. 17). It certainly has been "consistently linked" in papers like these; but such claims invite the question: Where is the proof? Despite a lot of talk about growth, I see no evidence for its claims.

For example, Hathaway says it is reasonable to believe that job creation ("employment growth") is "especially strong" for high-tech startups. But the only reason he gives is that the "presence" of venture capital investment in a region has been "causally linked" with "greater employment growth and income generation in the same region," simply citing another paper without saying clearly what the causal link might be (I suspect it is merely a statistical correlation and not a causal link at all.). The fact that creating one high-tech job is "associated" with four new jobs in the "local services economy" or R&D investment (taxpayer subsidies?) by high-tech firms hardly proves anything or justifies the implicit claim about high-tech startups and job creation. Which might explain the lukewarm conclusion of his last sentence on page 17: "Let's hope that 2011 was the beginning of a sustained revival in technology entrepreneurship and entrepreneurship overall." Not exactly confidence inspiring, particularly since this was written in 2013.

Given that "[f]ew new businesses will ever grow substantially or innovate" (p. 3), how "high-tech companies" can "play an outsized role in job creation" (p. 2) is anybody's guess. How "job-creation" among such startups can be so "robust" as to offset job losses across the board, when "the forces of job destruction were greater than the forces of job creation" (p. 2), leaves the reader in a quandary. How is it that distinguishing such startups from the rest can be important when "business dynamics data do not allow a clear distinction between growth-oriented "startups" and other new businesses"? This piece also advertises the idea that STEM training is an important job creator.

You can't have it both ways.

If Hathaway's paper is puzzling, Dane Stangler's *Path-Dependent Startup Hubs—Comparing Metropolitan Performance: High-Tech and ICT Startup Density*, another Kauffman Foundation effort of September 2013, is singularly uninspiring. Piggy-backing on Hathaway's "Tech Starts" paper, this piece, which purports to say something meaningful about "entrepreneurship ecosystems" (euphemistic jargon for "startup communities"), begins with the familiar assumption that these high-tech sectors are the job creators and "important drivers of economic growth" (p. 2). Along the way to reaching the earth-shaking conclusion that "no place can transform itself overnight," it shares such startling "observations" as "Startup density appears to be a path-dependent phenomenon" (that is, it follows a certain course) and "The most fertile source of entrepreneurial spawning is the population of existing companies." But its concluding paragraph is noteworthy for its candor, if nothing else:

> More work must be done to understand the local and regional dynamics of entrepreneurship, barriers that may exist to catalyzing a self-fulfilling dynamic of entrepreneurial spinoffs, and what the proper role of supporting institutions should be. Each metropolitan area deserves to be approached on its own terms, with an understanding of how local dynamics shape its entrepreneurial ecosystem.

In other words, they don't understand the "local and regional dynamics of entrepreneurship," or the barriers to "catalyzing a self-fulfilling dynamic of entrepreneurial spinoffs," or what the "proper role of supporting institutions should be." To approach cities "with an understanding of how local dynamics shape its entrepreneurial ecosystem" is fraught with the prior unsubstantiated assumption that any such thing as an "entrepreneurial ecosystem" even exists.

However, another effort of the Kauffman Foundation, *Neutralism and Entrepreneurship: The Structural Dynamics of Startups, Young Firms, and Job Creation* [Dane Stangler and Paul Kedrofsky, September 2010] offers a far more provocative performance than the preceding entries.

Exactly how "new and young companies" contribute to job creation, according to the authors, reflects (but only "partly") the "dynamics of firm accumulation" (which means: "how firms enter and exit or survive over time") and must be seen "in the proper structural context." One searches this paper in vain for anything amounting to a definition of these key terms, "dynamics of firm accumulation" and "proper structural context."

Once again the claim: "young firms and startups (less than five years old) account for most net new jobs." So what? This is neither surprising nor informative, since "net" implies those jobs created in excess of jobs lost. Since most businesses (including startups) fail within five years and older established firms do not create new jobs for obvious reasons of maintaining internal and financial stability, this also gives the lie to the myth of "growth" (p. 2).

Because the footnote offered in support of "this empirically established claim" (that is, the claim at the top of the previous paragraph) cites a government census "overview" with the impressive-sounding title of "Business Dynamics Statistics dataset," there is good reason to doubt the original assertion, at least to the extent that it is not simply tautological. The same footnote cites no fewer than four Kauffman Foundation "reports" and briefings, all front-loaded with rhetoric and pseudo-scientific jargon asserting the same claim, lacking any page references or specifics, which is no confirmation of anything except dreaming from an organization that styles itself "The Foundation of Entrepreneurship."

Page 2 hedges its bets about startups' contribution to the assumed job creation by mentioning that "their contribution must be seen in the proper structural context." —So: what is the proper structural context?

Asserting "the need for a more complete understanding of the dynamics of firm formation and job creation" only underscores the fact that they don't understand dynamics of firm formation and job creation.

To assuage this need and make up for their lack, Stangler and Kedrofsky seize upon Japanese biologist Motoo Kimura's "neutral theory of evolution," which "posited a baseline rate of mutation-driven change that, from the standpoint of genetic and physiological evolution, is largely neutral." Kimura's work focuses on stability rather than change. "Natural selection is a conservative force. It spends

35

more of its time keeping species the same than changing them." The theory is not only conservative, it supports the status quo. How convenient. Why, it is the perfect model for a putative theory of business dynamics! Especially one tailored to serve the interests of a multinational corporate power bloc.

Except that it isn't. Business is not biology, corporations are not persons and industries are not species. Kimura's theory of mutation and natural selection yields no credible empirical insight into or connections with corporations and business. To suggest otherwise is not science but a deplorable, facile and self-serving charade. Stangler and Kedrofsky admit they have no data, then adopt a metaphor from evolutionary biology, and finally infer that the high rate of business failure (and attendant massive unemployment)—i.e., "creative destruction"—is actually a force for stability and improvement. This kind of phony science is nothing more than a tortured defense of Social Darwinism. Specious. Facetious. Evidently, the "proper structural context" of any presumed "dynamic of firm accumulation" is simply the fact that some firms startup while others go out of business.

Consider the authors' spurious refutation of John Kenneth Galbraith:

> John Kenneth Galbraith, for example, excised the entrepreneur from economic progress in his 1967 book, *The New Industrial State*. No longer, would new firms and innovations create waves in the economy; rather, the "technostructure" of big companies and big government successfully managed both demand and supply and, thereafter, innovations would emerge from that structure.

Citing Intel's founding a year after Galbraith published, however, substantiates rather than undermines Galbraith's observation about innovations. In both *The Affluent Society* and *The New Industrial State*, Galbraith was talking about corporate consolidation and concentration of power and narrow interests, not trying to justify corporate capitalism by anointing entrepreneurialism as its Messiah.

Neutralism and Entrepreneurship quotes Dan Spulber's "simple yet profound observation" that "the entrepreneur's economic contribution is the creation of the firm itself." Wait a minute. What happened to the

36

frothy claims about Human Capital, STEM training and technological innovation driving the economy?

This report admittedly "constructs an imaginary economy to illustrate the structural dynamics of job creation." Yet, on page 19, the report "has yet to consider the importance of high growth firms in their structural context." That is the last time *Neutralism and Entrepreneurship* so much as mentions the term "structural context."

Extrapolating "imputed survival lines" to "see the dynamics of firm entry and exit" is imaginary and totally fabricated out of thin air. "Conceivably," the report qualifies, "most firms die at some point." That is no insight. After spinning an entire "imaginary economy" like gold from straw, why the dubious tone? Can Rumpelstiltskin keep from blurting out his secret?

The report posits an "assumed constancy of startup entry." That is quite an assumption. Or rather: the goal of some overall corporate state planning? The authors refer to "assumptions based on real data" (usually the best kind). Well, let's see.

The imaginary economy begins with "an empty landscape" then decides to "plug in" an "average" 500,000 imaginary new businesses along with "imputed survival rates" based on the "actual experience of the American economy" from 1977 through 2005 as measured by the BDS dataset. Not surprisingly, the actual model parallels ("tracks") assumptions made in their paper and imaginary economy. For example, young firms age 1-5 make up the "largest demographic sector" in any given year and reflect "a downward sloping business survival rate." Well, what do you expect? I mean: how "imaginary" can your extrapolated economy be if it uses the same data as a model that measures actual business performance?

On the other hand, taking pre-1977 firms into account (their ages unknown), the report finds that new and young firms cannot constitute the largest demographic bloc of firms in any given year because older companies outnumber them. On the same page, footnote # 25 muddies the definitional waters by calling into question the distinction between "young" and "old" firms ("Older" is "a relative term," we are told).

In 1977, the pre-1977 category of "older" firms included a large number of young companies from the previous five years—likely a plurality, in fact. On the other end, the age classifications of these data mean that any company age six and older is categorized, somewhat imprecisely, as old or at least not young.

Based on the extrapolated numbers of its imaginary economy, the report concludes "...the absolute number of firms younger than age five remains the same but constitutes a slightly decreasing proportion of the entire universe of firms. At the same time, however, *in any given year, young firms make up the largest cohort of all firms in the economy.* Even though, numerically, there will be a steadily greater volume of older firms, new and young firms will, proportionately, make up the largest bloc of firms." (My italcs) —That is one way to prove an assumption but it is based on a *nice*, that is, a casuistic distinction. To assume what you need to reach a desired conclusion may be a viable strategy in constructing deductive proofs in mathematical logic, but it is the epitome of bad empirical science. Stangler and Kedrofsky simply assume that young firms are the largest group of firms, implying that this is why they create the most new jobs, and assemble their data in patterns that appear to support those assumptions.

"Our imaginary economy is perpetually young." This, by the way, is a foundational principle of Kauffman-style entrepreneurial investment and an unquestioned assumption of the hypertrophic and hyperbolic MBA and EMBA programs described earlier.

When, describing its own projected data on page 7, the report asserts, "the pyramid of firms in any economy will look like this," the word choice is telling. That is exactly what this is: a pyramid or Ponsi scheme.

To say of this pyramid that it "echoes, and is perhaps a corollary of, the Zipf distribution of firm size," the authors have merely abducted a convenient piece of statistical jargon. For "this is not merely a restatement of the firm-size distribution." (It's not? Then what exactly is it that "echoes" the Zipf distribution?) This is followed by a confused piling up of platitudes and clichés ("most young firms are small," "not all small firms are young," some "young firms" grow big quickly,) that make no relevant or meaningful distinctions.

To assert of "job creation: it is embedded within this structure of firm entry and survival and accumulation" is tantamount to saying "job creation occurs within an economy." There is no "dynamics of firm formation" and no "proper structural context" beyond mere extrapolated projections. The whole edifice is sheer nonsense. The flimsiness of the paper's contentions is shown by its ludicrously sterile hint that job creation by new and young firms "could be, in part," a "function" of "the arithmetic of firm accumulation." I suppose that means counting the number of firms could have some relation to employment.

On page 12, things get worse, as blunder gives birth to bluster.

> There are clearly structural dynamics at work that help explain the provenance of new jobs. Quoting Robert Axtell: "The Zipf distribution...places important limits on models of firm dynamics."

The basis for this? "...new and young companies account for between 30 percent and 40 percent of all firms in the economy. This percentage naturally falls over time, albeit slowly, as the overall number of firms grows, but this demographic of firms is nonetheless a plurality each year, something that would persist over time..." In other words, the mere fact that new and young firms can be measured and compared with all other firms or subsets of firms proves that there are "structural dynamics at work that help explain the provenance of new jobs." Clearly, it does no such thing—not without a better idea of what the alleged structural dynamics are or how they operate to explain the genesis of job creation.

With "employment churn" (employee turnover and replacement), more jargon is introduced. Charged words like "birth" and "death" smuggle in the creepy notion that corporate change resembles biological evolution; which nevertheless indirectly confirms Hannah Arendt's contention that the biological life forces of "growth, metabolism, and eventual decay," the condition of human labor, have shaped modern society and its insistence that "life is the highest good."

For all its chatter about "the structural dynamics of firm accumulation," this report nowhere offers a coherent definition of "firm accumulation" or "structural dynamics," or confirms that these terms have any reference outside the nominal context of its own quasi-operationalist language. The claim about job creation comes down to this: "the preponderance of young firms in the economy raises the probability that a large contribution to job creation will come from these companies." The report is careful to deny that "market share or innovation or growth rates also follow the shape of accumulation set forth here." This report is forced to claim that no economy "operates in a deterministic fashion"—otherwise, what happens to that expansive free will central to the individualistic ideological component so vital to the myth of "free" market capitalism?

These provisos reveal the real sterility of this alleged "research."

> It is important to note what this analysis is *not* saying. We are not claiming that the distribution of performance indicators like market share or innovation or growth rates also follow the shape of accumulation set forth here.

That is a fatal disclaimer. If "performance indicators" like "market share or innovation or growth rates" do not "follow the shape of accumulation set forth here," then what is the point of focusing on the "dynamics of firm accumulation" in the first place? Wasn't the analysis supposed to show something about productivity?

What becomes of the hypothesized "structural dynamics"? Wasn't this the framework that was supposed to explain institutional behavior? The "structural features" are easily overlooked, the report avers, because they are "structurally embedded." This jargony "embedded" recalls its use in another context: that of journalists embedded with the military in Iraq and Afghanistan. I suspect it serves a similar purpose in *Neutralism and Entrepreneurship*: that of subterfuge.

But what are they, these "structural features"? The only proof offered is buried in footnote # 48:

> "In general, incorporating turnover into traditional industrial organization clarifies how underlying structure shapes the environment in which market outcomes are determined."

—I don't see how. Moreover, merely citing a 1998 paper in the *Journal of Economic Literature* (the source of the footnoted quote) does nothing to clarify things, either.

"Without understanding them," that is, structural features, the paper goes on to conclude [Yes, this is the paper's "Conclusion: What Do the Underlying Dynamics Mean?" Surely, the wrong place to be asking that question], "we could very well undermine them and thus lose the job-creating benefits of new and young companies." —You mean the ones that your report has already repeatedly called into question and nullified?

"New and young companies do indeed account for most net job creation in the U.S. economy, but this is due, in part, to their status as the largest demographic category of companies."

—This is the whole of the claim and the evidence for the claim in the same package.

The obsession with job-creating startups and structural dynamics is irresistible, as the following quotes from the "Conclusion" show.

That job-creation "also reflects a host of factors aside from the firm itself" presents "a suggestive line of future research that falls out of this paper," says footnote # 50. "Falls out of this paper" is about right. Does it mean "falls outside the scope of this paper"? (I nearly fell out, myself, when I read it.) Referencing the 1998 paper mentioned above, footnote # 43 "should call into question the conventional definition of economic growth as simply more products or services or revenues." If economic growth does not necessarily involve more commodities, services and revenues, what does it involve: less?

However, the mere fact that job-creation reflects many factors besides firms

> ...should not denigrate the importance of new and young companies and the jobs they create.

Who said anything about denigrating them? After all,

> ...the reality of firm dynamics presented here is premised on certain truths that are not immutable: a more or less steady

inflow of startups; more or less consistent survival rates from
year to year."

—Which truths are "not immutable"? Oh, that's right: *empirical
truths,* that is, scientific knowledge. Covertly reminding us that
Neutralism and Entrepreneurship constitutes real, bona fide science, a
"steady flow of startups" and "consistent survival rates," if not
immutable, certainly resemble empirical generalizations. But they are
unanchored to any substantive data. Being too mutable pretty much
cancels the assumed "reality of firm dynamics."

Or maybe not. The "dynamics of firm accumulation" underscoring
"the overriding importance of firm formation to economic growth" are
to be understood "not in any revolutionary sense, but in the neutralist
sense of a steady baseline beat of firm entry and exit, a structural
premise of which other economic phenomena are incidents." Get it?
Like an itchy poisonwood rash you can't keep from scratching, despite
the pain and burning, the vision of an endless profusion of new
businesses with the regularity of a healthy heartbeat is irresistible.
("And the Beat Goes On…" Sing it, Sonny and Cher.) Precisely what
the Kauffman Foundation, graduate MBA programs and investors
want to conclude to justify their strategy for "growing" consumption
and aggregate GDP, keep the money flowing through the banking
system, and upward to the 1%. By keeping everybody in constant flux
under the illusion that they too can become a billionaire or at least a
millionaire, the report slyly admits between the lines or in the fine
print of this bogus research that "creative destruction" (large business
failures and recurrent waves of unemployment) is the expected norm,
while at the same time pretending to show the exact opposite.

No occurrence of the terms "structural dynamics" or "dynamics"
offers so much as the hint of a formal definition. Despite their
continual association of job creation with notions of firm formation
and accumulation, entry, exit and survival of companies, no attempt is
made to fit the undefined terms into an overall theoretical scheme. Yet,
on page 17, these authors have the temerity to suggest that their
whimsical associations (they call them "variables") "resemble a
mathematical function, or at least a matter of higher probability"
(Higher than what?), which contradicts an assertion made on the
previous page: "the reality of firm dynamics presented here…should

42

not be seen as functions of mathematical inevitability—they are the *reasons behind* the mathematical probabilities described here." Which is it: a mathematical probability or the reason behind the probability?

The coup de grâce is revealing:

> ...there would seem to be a relationship between the *a priori* level of firm formation, the ensuing structural dynamics, and the subsequent emergence of high-growth firms.

Seem, seeming, seamy. Take that "ensuing structural dynamics": ensuing from what, an "*a priori* level of firm formation"? But *a priori* means "prior to experience," "analytic," "not supported by fact"; by definition, unempirical. She-loves-me, she-loves-me-not. This see-sawing between what is (only alleged) and what may be (but we don't actually know yet) is enough to induce permanent motion-sickness. But it was the report's burden to provide evidence for the assumed relationship.

Because Stangler and Kedrofsky are as unable to explain the emergence of high-growth firms as they are to define structural dynamics, they must make the former seem "less interesting" by subsuming it under the (equally undefined) notions of "healthy levels of firm entry, exit, and inter-firm productivity reallocation," which they imply justifies invoking a "Pareto distribution" to explain the "resulting picture of firm performance." But a Pareto distribution can't explain high-growth firm performance if the Pareto distribution is premised on the very elements that condition performance of high-growth firms in the first place. That is what is called a circular definition.

This whole rigamarole is larded with repetition ad nauseum of exactly this kind of unconfirmed (and probably unconfirmable) claim. The claim itself is so flakey that the report can walk away from it without any sense of hypocrisy or inconsistency, as the following admissions show:

> ...structural order should not be overplayed and may actually point in a direction away from the firm as the analytical locus of job creation.

We should not accept or try to understand this reality in terms of a "just so" narrative—as if it is perfectly natural that new and young firms contribute most net new jobs because they are seen as somehow superior to older and larger companies.

Yet this is precisely the narrative "obsession" that the authors do accept and report as established fact. Does "just so" denote the adverb (meaning "in a careful manner")? Or is it an unconscious reference to Kipling's "Just So" stories in which fanciful answers are given to questions like why the leopard has spots or the elephant a trunk? Either interpretation undermines the report's credibility. In spite of having earlier ruled determinism out of the economic picture it tried to paint by denying that "the American economy or any economy operates in a deterministic fashion," the report now tells us that the claim should raise "the issue of causality in economic change." But which claim is being referred to here? The claim of an undefined structural dynamics, the assumed claims about firm formation, or the tenuous one about startups creating the most jobs?

We get more jargon: "inter-firm productivity reallocation...a Pareto distribution." Not surprisingly, such a distribution is "premised on the structure of firm formation, exit, and accumulation." This supposedly confirms the alleged neutralist model. "[I]f high-growth firms and the job creation record of new and young companies are partly incidents of these underlying dynamics, then we can see the process of economic selection and propagation acting upon this important baseline of firms being created and accumulating over time." That's a big *if* and a convoluted way of begging the question. (If wishes were horses, then beggars would ride...) All this really amounts to is a pathetic demand: *Maximize startups. Keep 'em coming. The more, the merrier.*

Here is the naked program, plan and agenda: "...there is an evolution underway in risk capital markets. The emergence of professional, seed-centric acceleration programs (e.g., TechStars, Y Combinator, Betaworks, etc.) has made it easier for a larger amount of company creation experimentation to take place. Rather than requiring $3 million to $5 million in investment, and then $100 million and larger exits, these smaller funding groups will invest as little $50,000, thus requiring much smaller exits for profitable returns..." This sounds like damage control for addicted gamblers.

By Jobs! It is the self-fulfilling prophecy of Kauffman ("The Foundation of Entrepreneurship")! "...a structural change [is] underway in the rate at which new companies are created in the United States."

Don't forget the necessary complement to that steady base line beat of corporate growth, namely, "creative destruction": "...a higher level of firm creation should bring with it a higher level of failure—and this will be a good thing."

But...for *whom* will it be "a good thing"—employees who lose their jobs—and what remediation, compensation or redress for this mixed blessing do these mavens and mouthpieces of corporate industry propose? None at all. What the analysis "seems" to suggest "is the existence of a dual microeconomic structure beneath the aggregate picture of job creation. The first is the structure outlined here; the second is the dynamic of churn among firms and individuals across all sectors." —I've heard some pretty rank bullshit in my 64 years, but this takes the cake. One waits with baited breath for these "experts" to discover an underlying dynamical quantum reality that will enable them to make on the fly pronouncements about subatomic micro-particles of the economy.

X. Economics as Pseudo-Science

In 1974, Paul A. Samuelson published this advice in *The Journal of Portfolio Management*:

> A respect for evidence compels me to incline toward the hypothesis that most portfolio decision makers should go out of business—take up plumbing, teach Greek, or help produce the annual GNP by serving as corporate executives. Even if this advice to drop dead is good advice, it obviously is not counsel that will be eagerly followed. Few people will commit suicide without a push.

Mandelbrot and Hudson quote Samuelson's advice in *The (mis)Behavior of Markets*, cited earlier. Mandelbrot, a true entrepreneur (he invented fractal geometry), writes:

> We lurch from crisis to crisis. In a networked world, mayhem in one market spreads instantaneously to all others—and we have only the vaguest of notions how this happens, or how to regulate it. So limited is our knowledge that we resort, not to science, but to shamans. We place control of the world's largest economy in the hands of a few elderly men, the central bankers.

Mandelbrot approvingly quotes financial analyst and entrepreneur Richard Olsen: "We literally know nothing about how economics works."

Actually, we know a great deal about how economics works, and how financial markets work. Or don't work. It comes to the same thing in the case of modern multinational corporate capitalism, the monetary-market system for which it stands, and their self-interested social science propagandists of money value. Unfortunately, this knowledge is reflected neither in what business schools and economics departments teach nor in the loopy concoctions of so-called corporate leaders and executives. Virtually all of these individuals, including the social scientists, are committed ideologues, that is, believers in what we might call the standard model of unlimited progress, expansive free will, total individual responsibility (of humans, not corporations), the "free market," what historians call "the gospel of wealth and success," salvation through technology, and innovation (defined at whim according to the definitional standard implied or imposed by the preceding notions). Mostly, they believe in profit-maximization as sole arbiter and standard of all social value, of morality, of truth, even of civilization itself. Most of all, they believe in CYA where their own employment and advancement is concerned. Do you begin to see a structural dynamic here?

Although economics can be made more scientific (that is, can be held to a legitimate standard of scientific knowledge), economics will never magically transform itself into a true predictive science. For what is missing is the genuine source of the complexity, that is, the political dimension of opinion and human action with its features of "the unpredictability of its outcome, the irreversibility of the process, and the anonymity of its authors." Hannah Arendt called this "the three-fold frustration of action": it is the source of the human temptation of

> seeking shelter from action's calamities in an activity where one man, isolated from all others, remains master of his doings from beginning to end. This attempt to replace acting with making is manifest in the whole body of argument against "democracy," which, the more consistently and better reasoned it is, will turn into an argument against the essentials of politics.

That project convulsed corporate capitalism throughout the nineteenth century. Sweeping up the nation in a romantic frenzy that blended religion, law, science and technology, corporate capitalists pursued a delusional agenda, subjugating the continent. Obsessed by reconstructing the natural world through steam, rail, canals and wireless telegraphy, the nation was blinded to the divisive issues that would erupt in the Civil War. That agenda has lasted and intensified through the twentieth century down to our present permanent war economy, national security surveillance state, and the looming threat of supranational corporate governance via the Trans-Pacific Partnership and Trade-in-Services Agreements. That multinational corporate capitalism has come so near to achieving this terrifying goal should motivate citizens to forge a permanent, nationwide system of autonomous town meetings to mobilize, spearhead and consolidate concerted action for changes that meet the besetting challenges of global warming, international fascism, massive unemployment and forced migration.

"When it comes to measuring risk," Mandelbrot argues, "the industry's toolkit is surprisingly bare. The two most common tools are α, or volatility, and β, or the degree to which a stock's price changes correlate to those of the market overall." These are used over and over, Mandelbrot says, "the latter in portfolio construction and corporate finance, the former in virtually every kind of risk calculation under the sun." Bad science: when your only tool is a hammer, every problem looks like a nail.

Describing predictive gambits like the Monte Carlo simulation in modern economics as "a computational nightmare," Mandelbrot goes on to describe some of the other rattletraps, rattlesnakes and time bombs. "Valuing options correctly is a high-roller game, but the rules are all messed up." The "most widely known formula" based on the 1973 work of Fischer Black and Myron Scholes, Mandelbrot asserts, "is simply wrong. It makes unrealistic assumptions."

A big problem is the "assumption of constant volatility—in essence, that the world does not change. If Black-Scholes were right, this would be a very boring picture, one flat line for all the varieties." Mandelbrot says there is no consensus among economists which, if any of the many attempts to fix the formula, works best. "In the absence of clear answers, it has become a case of every man for himself."

As noted earlier regarding the vagaries of claims about "creating value," Mandelbrot writes that "there are no good valuation formulae."

Citing six financial crises that destabilized currencies and produced a wave of bankruptcies in the late 1990s and noting "what passed for investment research before (the bubble burst) was not only wrong, but fraudulent," this theorist urges "wise leadership." But "wise leadership" is hardly a known, let alone a reliable, quantity. While "investments from others" might magnify the Wall Street settlement's impact, it is far more likely to stimulate fraud and shortsighted profiteering than prove conducive to planetary and global benefit. And that is no hypothesis or estimate but is born out by the entire record.

A "coordinated search for patterns in financial markets" is a Holy Grail, a mirage and delusion. Economics is grounded in inherently unpredictable human psychology, emotions, politics, culture, in short *in everything within the system* of both our fabricated world of artifacts and the biosphere. Modern multinational capitalism seeks to merge these two "worlds" in order to reduce them to a standard model of behavioral predictability, which will ultimately result in the destruction of both worlds. Advertising is built on fraud, deception, manipulation and lies. Most behavioral social science depends on the tools and models of advertising and modern marketing, and is intrinsically contaminated thereby.

Economics is not a science and never can be; if, however, through a form of high-tech brainwashing (advertising) you can reduce human populations to submissive conformity in mass (market) behavior, even while feeding them enough mobile media distractions, pharmaceutical exhilarants and euphorics to convince them that they are the "luckiest, happiest, free-est" people in history, the rulers may be able to fool them into accepting economics as a true science. But not for long, I suspect. If you grind the inherent unpredictability, spontaneity, irreversibility, and anonymity of the human capacity for action—our very natality—out of existence, then you may be able to produce something resembling a science. But it will not be a science that "does not harm," as Benoit Mandelbrot imputes to pragmatism. (Aesculapius' "oath" does not rule all physicians; and it does not even partially define any philosophy of pragmatism that I know of.) And it will not be satisfying.

My intuition tells me that VIX (volatility) is probably a function of profit-maximization, or its distribution over time. But precisely how to describe that function and time scale? Is there a simpler way to describe or transform profit-maximization (profit-seeking)? Assumption: you don't have to find some magic number or equation...

As long as social science (economics, behavioral sciences, sociology) serves principles of capitalism as defined and interpreted by multinational corporate culture—oligarchic corporate culture—it will never be able to reverse the widening inequality of haves and have nots, that is, it will simply provide Wall Street and the executive barony with the means and methods for pursuing unfair advantage and profits to the detriment of the world, humankind and nature. This will be true of an economics based on multifractality, just as it has been true of every practical scientific application and technological advance in human history.

XI. Rattletraps, Rattlesnakes & Time Bombs

Of course the multinational corporate sector has quite a different narrative that they vigorously promote, convincing people that they can have their cake and eat it too. Mandelbrot calls this "the underlying message of modern portfolio theory." This, by the way, is something the American people have always deeply wanted to believe, sometimes referred to as the American Dream or American Way of Life (necessarily ignoring the entire history of capitalism).

But there is a problem with all of this, not a fly in the ointment, but rather an institutional Ebola virus that will infect corporations in the long run, and multinational conglomerates in particular. Given capitalism's consistent track record, even if enough high-tech startups could succeed in exploding consumption (not likely), any gains will be outweighed by the far greater number of economic and environmental rattletraps, rattlesnakes and time bombs that unregulated corporate frenzy is sure to spawn.

Corporate capitalism demands continuous if not accelerating consumption. This is the reason, the only reason, for pushing the doctrine and practice of technological salvation and entrepreneurship: it needs a reliable flow of customers to buy more of its stuff.

The antinomies and contradictions inherent in such stratagems are fatal to the whole scheme. Let me detail them now.

This vision of entrepreneurial humanity is based on two basic assumptions: that everyone is an entrepreneur or can learn to become one (not only false but fatuous) and that large corporations require continuous consumption in order to continue to profit through growth and diversification (true and a virtual tautology). The best way to achieve the second goal is by securing a continuous supply of consumers, for which a steady stream of entrepreneurial small businesses might seem at first the ideal solution. Equating "creative destruction" with progress and embracing boundless privatization, consigning non-exporting small businesses to a crowd-funding fate, sacrificing the public schools to provide real estate, construction, private testing and management companies with new sources of revenue: all exemplify ways in which profit-maximizing drives predatory capitalist parasitism.

51

According to the catechisms of entrepreneurial ideology, acquiescence in schemes like the one laid out in the Kauffman Report will bring success and happiness to everyone in the world, ultimately eliminating poverty and hunger, thereby ushering in an earthly paradise for all to enjoy.

Two problems render this pipe dream dead on arrival. One: It is essentially a pyramid or Ponsi scheme, often accompanied by that disparity between inflated stock price and actual value economists call *bubbles*. Two: If everyone becomes an entrepreneur, who exactly is going to perform the work or labor upon which capitalist profits depend?

Only two possible answers occur to me. Perhaps machines rather than humans *will* perform all or virtually all of the labor necessary in the future. Although scientists have been predicting the mechanization of labor for over 100 years, it is hard to see how we might actually arrive at this stage, given that capitalism is by definition, and in theory as well as practice, the exploitation of cheap labor in order to create profits for the principals or shareholders.

Of course, anything approximating complete automation imperils organized labor's very existence. It is well known that construction is the most dangerous and wasteful industry. Nearly 20% of all fatalities in private industry in 2012 were in construction. To confirm the inefficiency and waste of materials, visit any construction site and look at the dumpsters filled with lumber and other building materials left behind. Experts have proposed how gigantic 3-D printers programmed for residential and commercial construction could eliminate both deficiencies of human labor. So ideally and rationally, we should celebrate the demise of human labor in this arena and its replacement by automation.

So what are you going to do with the resulting massive unemployed population? I submit that neither capitalism (which has never in 400 years been able to provide meaningful work or a decent standard of living for the majority of citizens) nor socialism (which is inevitably tied to capitalism through its dependence on capital and the monetary-market system) has any practicable answer.

The second possibility is—following the Kauffman Foundation's example—failure to create any actually successful small businesses to match their rhetorical boasts about entrepreneurship will force all entrepreneurs to get into the education business in some form or other. Entrepreneurs themselves will presumably be educated, if not in the STEM disciplines then in the *science of entrepreneurship* in (which they will all surely be adepts by that time). The entrepreneurs of privatization approve only of STEM subjects and teach them in their charter schools, because—they believe—only *these subjects* can possibly lead to the kind of technological innovations with new commercial applications that will guarantee future consumption, profits, growth and diversification. Of course, such pedagogical consolidation could go hand-in-hand with the mechanization of practically all work and labor.

Anyone who knows anything about technology and education knows that innovation never occurs in a vacuum, let alone the restrictive positivist environment of STEM training. Scientific discoveries of the kind that lead to meaningful innovations and intelligible patents require a robustly dynamic context of the liberal arts and sciences in which free inquiry, experimentation and new ideas can germinate. Scientific ideas often have non-scientific sources.

Of course, the more plausible reading here is that entrepreneurial capitalism's alleged concern for education is simply a ruse. On this account, the last thing corporations want are educated citizens who might question their legitimacy, goals, policies and practices. What they crave are gullible, malleable consumers, docile employees and, in case of workforce glut, obedient soldiers who will die quietly in capitalism's inevitable wars.

The June 2014 "Prosperity at a Crossroads" overgrown broadsheet recommends more deregulation, privatizing public education, replacing traditional content with STEM training and "core" curricula, redrawing state and regional boundaries, expropriating state and federal treasuries, rewriting patent law, transforming cities and towns into mega-cities conducive to high-tech export trade and high-rolling investors. Small businesses unable to export their goods or services to foreign markets like India and China (that is, most small businesses) are advised to launch online websites and look into crowd-funding as a means of generating revenue. There isn't going to be any money left over for them when the multinational corporate vacuum cleaner is done sucking up all the loose capital, currency and change in America, not to mention the rest of the world. Look at Detroit and Ferguson, or Greece, or all the bankrupt cities in America for a glimpse of the future. Better yet, look at Iraq and Afghanistan—if you want to see what the corporate endgame will look like for the majority of people in the United States. To quote the late Nobel laureate Richard Feynman: "The whole thing is rotten."

Given the Pentagon and U.S. Space Command "Vision for 2020" with its plans for "Full Force Integration" and "Full Spectrum Dominance," recent events (for example, a permanent state of war, proliferating weaponized drones, and resumption of neo-conservative and neo-liberal Cold War tactics toward Russia) force me to conclude that the U.S. fully intends to take control of the planet by dominating space with superior (probably nuclear) weapons. Make no mistake: it is supranational corporate conglomerate interests that are spearheading all of this in a drive to further consolidate their global hegemony. They believe that confiscating all capital assets for their own use will advance that goal.

Written exclusively from the viewpoint of high-roller investors and corporate executives, what "Prosperity" makes abundantly clear is that this master plan does not include most of the middle class, workers, the poor, the young, the old, or minorities. The blueprint for "progress" will replace the educational system with STEM training in a misguided effort to stimulate innovation and siphon off the workers it needs; the rest of the population is on its own. The proposed Trans-Pacific Partnership and Trade in Services agreements grant the Petrochemical Cartel and other conglomerates unfettered license to pursue their goals with impunity, immune to any regulation not of their own making. No wonder the corporate bloc wants Congress to grant Obama fast track authority to ram this into law. But the corporate program has larger, more dangerous ambitions.

The exceptionalist entrepreneurial ideology is fatal to local resilience, political autonomy, and community Rights of Nature, for it endorses a profit-maximizing, multinational, corporate paradigm as the ultimate solution for the entire world. This paradigm underwrites the status quo

54

of fossil fuel, nuclear power and petrochemicals; it drives and informs corporate capitalism's plan to reshape and redesign the entire surface of the earth and to replace every sovereign nation, its government and laws with the paradigm's own multinational superstructure.

To cement these goals, the multinationals require a highly mobile pool of low-wage workers (de facto slaves) they can deploy around the world at will. This explains their need to transcend the newly dismantled client nation-states and fill the resulting vacuum with their own governing "authority." They especially long to rewrite the laws governing all aspects of human social life on the planet, including environmental integrity, public health, reproductive and women's rights, worker safety, pharmaceuticals, banking, scientific research and technological innovation, patent law, internet and net neutrality, community rights, rights of nature, criminal and civil law. These are in fact the goals that the Trans-Pacific Partnership Agreement and Trade-in-Services Agreement will achieve, if implemented.

We must not allow this to happen. The only viable alternative, as I see it, is for local communities comprising municipalities and townships to organize and consolidate their efforts in a campaign of nonviolent noncooperation, civil disobedience, and intervention. Strategic efforts designed to galvanize the nation should be coordinated toward achieving a single, clearly articulated, overarching goal: that of permanently dismantling all multinational corporations and submitting all corporate entities to coherent regulatory authority based on the principles and practice of democratic political rule.

Lewis Powell's 1971 "Memo" or "Manifesto" to The U.S. Chamber of Commerce was the blueprint for the subsequent exaltation of corporate vested interests leading up to their expropriation of personhood along with other Constitutional rights, the advent of Dark Money, the *Citizens United* and *McCutcheon* decisions in the Supreme Court. The epitome of a corporate lawyer, appointed to the Supreme Court by President Richard Nixon shortly after composing his "Manifesto," Powell was utterly convinced that big business was under siege by the forces of democracy. Besides advocating that corporations covertly infiltrate media, college and university campuses for the purpose of influencing education itself with pro-corporate business propaganda, Powell proposed a political litmus or "loyalty" test to identify a staff of highly qualified scholars in the social sciences who were true believers in the corporate capitalist system.

XII. Equality is America's Identity, Not a Brand

In *Thomas Jefferson The Art of Power* (2012), Jon Meacham documented how our third and arguably most influential American President had good reason to fear the monarchical aspirations of Federalists like Alexander Hamilton. Opposed to this perceived oligarchic threat to the young democracy, Thomas Jefferson energetically promoted and fiercely defended a democratic republic based upon the *political equality* of all citizens. A stubborn anti-democratic streak in America originated with the Puritans, though not all Puritans drew the same conclusions from the fears associated with "leveling." As I recount in *Sinister Dynamic*, Roger Williams rejected outright European claims to the land of indigenous people in the New World; and *he did so* on religious and theological grounds! A century later, Jonathan Edwards would find that simple uneducated persons were more likely than the learned to possess the wisdom and grace needed to recognize what threatens the state and the welfare of society. (Edward Snowden doesn't exactly have a Ph.D. from Stanford or MIT, yet his grasp of what matters morally like his ability to apply moral principles is unimpaired). Both Hannah Arendt and Edwards recognized (what Perry Miller found) in the human capacity for judgment

> a taste or relish that discerns "without being at the trouble of a train of reasoning," and therefore is always accessible to the democracy. For the mass of men, unread in historical monographs, "the evidence they can have from history, cannot be sufficient," but usually, the more men study history, the more they acquire doubts.

"Everything in our government and our society," wrote David Dudley Field in 1855, "proceeds from the idea of equality." Equality "not of strength, nor of genius, nor of external circumstances, but in rights and essential attributes," Field wrote, "abases none but elevates all." Field called equality "the peculiar doctrine of the American people, their ornament, their glory, the foundation of their strength, and the chief source of their prosperity."

This "idea of equality," Field realized, was nothing less than America's national identity. An exceptional jurist of the 19th century,

Field advocated a system of codification that would simplify American law by removing the confusion which forced judges into legislating; a method and system that would allow judges to cite the law itself rather than cases by applying statutes, a law based "upon principle rather than precedent," and rid the profession of pettifogging shysters. Perry Miller called Field the most "conservative" of the lot when it came to the relation of the law to property: "The primary purpose of the law, he wrote, is to govern property." Not *protect* it behind gated communities, police barricades, weaponized drones armed militias.

Today, in the 21st century, we are still fighting the same battle for equality as Jefferson and Field; only our monarchical adversary has a Multinational Corporate face: the implacable stare of the Petrochemical Cartel and the Fossil Fuel Conglomerate, ALEC and the NRA, keystroke liquidation of private property and banksters' gambles with taxpayers' dollars.

It remains to be seen whether local communities can summon the political will to act and restore democratic control of the *res publica* with a full complement of institutions, including media, education, science, family, art, religion, and gender. To do so, they will have to bring disparate, often isolated members of the community together into a deliberative decisional council system of political equals. To be effective, they will have to coordinate their organizing and planning with as many other municipal communities throughout the country as they can muster. Hannah Arendt has eloquently described the theoretical framework, particular passions, and standards required if local communities want to rediscover "the lost treasure of the revolutions," namely, authentic political freedom experienced by directly participating in governance to reconcile issues of equality and legitimate authority. Gene Sharp has provided the tools in his 100-page manual, *From Dictatorship to Democracy: A Conceptual Framework for Liberation* (The Albert Einstein Institution, 2010). This work is freely available online as a .pdf download at http://www.aeinstein.org/).

The extent to which sustained local political activity should be covert and private or transparent and public under conditions of a national security surveillance state is a highly relevant issue. Citizens must decide based on the nature and content of the campaign goals and strategies they adopt. Given the long history of American corporate and judicial hostility to labor organizing and the more recent police suppression of the Occupy Wall Street movement, it is reasonable to ask whether organized activists can actually establish physical spaces as venues for assembly and deliberation that do not threaten the powers-that-be and trigger violent police repression. The presence of older adults (50 years and up), women, children, and "solid citizens" representing small businesses and neighborhoods, organized labor, Muslim, Jewish and Christian churches, Native Americans, Whites, African Americans and Latinos could galvanize a community and capture the attention of elected officials. I do not think that police will shoot down citizens in the street for protesting the status quo or exercising their Constitutional right of assembly, especially if the protesting group includes a wide cross-section of citizens; but I may well be wrong about this. For the oligarchic establishment to commit violence against the popular citizenry, however, would prove a fatal mistake likely only to harden the protesting public's political will and intensify citizen resolve to achieve meaningful change.

Supranational capitalism inescapably driven by profit-maximization based on growing debt and consumption is unsustainable. The only way it can maintain even an illusion of promising futures for a majority is by subjecting citizens to a permanent, relentless, arbitrary, and unpredictable churn of technologies and innovation requiring endless re-education and retooling for an ever-shrinking and increasingly specialized range of careers. That terminal decisions about the content and character of such technologies and careers will be made exclusively on the basis of profit-maximization, instrumental utilitarian calculations, and marketing preferences should give no one comfort. This is a recipe for institutionalized cataclysm and societal chaos, not stability, certainly not prosperity (except for the few); neither conservative nor liberal but radical in the worst possible sense: by extracting profits for a tiny minority at the expense of the majority of citizens, it condones and perpetuates a system of slavery.

Why should everyone work for money? Why should everyone have to work at STEM-trained pursuits prescribed by corporate culture simply to maintain a system of capitalism that cannot create meaningful work or a decent standard of living for the majority of its citizens? Why continue to prop up such a sorry system? What can we do to put the economy on a sound foundation that minimizes or eliminates structural inequality?

The existing capitalist system promises to control populations through permanent war, unremitting destruction, and the spread of disease; to solve unemployment by means of forced evictions and migrations, a proliferating military and a privatized prison-industrial complex; to guarantee freedom and security by censoring media, suppressing genuine education, and arbitrarily deciding what is to count as scientific research and innovation. If this is the best we can do with a monetary-market system, why not scrap money, multiple currencies, and capital altogether? After all, we could replace them with unlimited, nonreciprocal, idiosyncratic credit—that is, credit from which the profit motive has been detached *by design*—and make it universally available to every person on the planet. This would eliminate poverty altogether, not just reduce it to an "acceptable" level that sacrifices millions in the process. It would also achieve the peaceful redistribution of goods and services worldwide without triggering economic implosion in developed countries and civil war in less developed ones; substituting for our present deluge of money-based problems (crime, drugs, human trafficking, war, etcetera) the much simpler one of managing global populations and resources. Birth control and family planning are far superior to cyclical famine and perpetual war for achieving this purpose.

At the very least, we could put the planet on a single standard of currency (I recommend solar or e-credits), eliminating the indeterminacy, unstable boom-and-bust cycles, and inherent destruction on which capitalism's opportunistic conglomerate banksters and "built-to-loot" rogue corporate pirates depend. We could subsidize Social Security and Medicare, probably education too, entirely through quantitative easing—I mean: it's not like our senior citizens are going to "take it with them." It will all go back into the economy.

Of course, replacing money with universal credit is not something that the U.S. or any other nation can accomplish unilaterally or by fiat. No, such an undertaking will require the cooperation and agreement of the entire planet. Making the effort will provide a real opening for

60

negotiating and adjusting the authentic interests that are common to every nation, country, tribe and person. The community of nations, including indigenous peoples, must be enlisted in this collective enterprise.

A shifting away from centralized banking, fossil fuel-based, global transportation systems of trade and toward decentralized, autonomous, locally resilient communitarian commerce is taking place under our noses. We need to face up to the colossal and abject failures of the wars on drugs and terror, to the significance of widespread homelessness and joblessness in America. While redesigning our economic institutions, we can afford to care for the nation's wounded veterans, ill served by the last several regimes. We can provide safe respectable housing and establish municipal communal kitchens and cafeterias to feed the homeless and indigent, young, old or displaced among our citizens. But doing so is incompatible with, and will never take place given, the profit-driven, Social Darwinist, selfish status quo that capitalism inevitably breeds. All that is wanting is the political will for concerted public action. Every elected official that degrades our political heritage by accusing opponents of "playing politics" should be stripped of office at once, tied up in bundles of six, and cast into the outer darkness. Every corporate executive and lobbyist who inflames that harm should be treated likewise.

Instead of mass unemployment, crime and starvation, why not implement universal credit for all, providing every person with the opportunity and resources to alternate one to five year periods of education, travel and self-development with shifts performing the work needed to maintain a functioning society? Humans need meaningful work to contribute to their community, the larger society and the world; they do not need to work for money or to "earn" their living. The need for trade, agriculture, creative arts and investigation in the sciences will persist; but these activities do not require global transportation, gigantic cargo ships and reconstructed seaports, mega-cities, the dismantling of sovereign nations and the rule of law, their subjugation and subservience to supranational corporate tyranny.

All of the human needs required for ecological sustainability can be satisfied at the local level of regional municipalities; these may well have to be reorganized and even scaled down to a manageable human size for the sake of population and practicalities. A clear-eyed recognition of the need for more community-shared public goods like internet, education, transportation, media and governance will inevitably replace consumption-driven materialism with its insatiable need to maximize individual ownership of commodities because it will restore to all the one good that modern capitalism can least afford: namely, time. By liberating one's time from its enslavement to the demands of capital and labor, citizens will enjoy the freedom to discover their true work, along with their identity and relationship to community. International trade will persist but no longer dominate the world or "the realm of human affairs" as it has in the past. If an economic system that is destroying the planet and killing off its people by the tens and hundreds of thousands cannot even provide decent work and living standards for the majority of citizens, doesn't it make sense to abolish that system in an orderly fashion and place lives and future on a better foundation?

> "He who would fix the pattern of decision by confining the American choice to one and only one mode of response—whether this be in politics, diplomacy, economics, literary form, or morality itself—such a one, in the light of our history, is the "truly Un-American."

The way to full employment is through full *un*employment—that is, rationally managed unemployment that repudiates the conditions of capitalism and the monetary-market anti-economy for which it stands.

It comes down to a choice that every citizen has to make individually, but all citizens will have to live with. If you really think that fossil fuel-driven, multinational corporate hegemony is going to create a good life for the vast majority of people on this planet, including a majority of U.S. citizens, then you might as well keep playing with your iPhones and mobile devices and let the collective ascendance to paradise unfold. I have tried to present some of the reasons why no one should accept this option. You must ignore the entire history of capitalism (more than 400 years in which exploitation, war, slavery, genocide, unemployment and bankruptcy have been the chief consequences). You must overlook the benumbed strategies of intimidation, manipulation, bullying, deceit and misdirection displayed by the Kauffman Report, its studied neglect of the needs of ordinary workers and the community, and its shrugging acceptance of predictable mass unemployment resulting from automation.

If, on the other hand, you find that permanent global governance by a supranational corporate hegemony, whose power dwarfs that of local communities and nation-states alike, is morally reprehensible, what choice do you have but to join the movement for local resilience and democratic authority? That movement is sweeping this country and uniting persons across a broad spectrum of age, ethnicity, class, education, gender and religion to regenerate American society in ways that reconcile equality and authority, that realign its practices and commitments with its ethos and principles. Some of the issues uniting these transformative energies include: food security, fracking, public education, alternatives to money and centralized banking, rights of nature to exist, and the right of communities to pass enforceable ordinances that strip corporations of an imputed right to engage in farming or any other activity that threatens the health and safety of citizens.

We are going to have to reinvigorate our local communities by rediscovering the freedom inherent in shared authentic organizing and genuine political experience. In the end, we will have to completely dismantle all multinational and transnational corporations if we expect to recover control of our democracy and save the earth for posterity. The all-powerful advertising, public relations, and marketing conglomerates will probably have to be dismantled first, their industries judiciously and comprehensively regulated. They are even more powerful and, in the long run, more dangerous than the "Too Big to Save" banks. Lobbying as we have known it will have to go. The responsibility for this will fall on every local community. Let's face it: profit-maximization, egotism, and instrumental utility are not very good yardsticks for measuring progress much less governing a world. Bertrand Russell was right: we have chosen "overwork for some and starvation for others" instead of "ease and security for all" but we the people did not choose these ends; they were chosen for us by those whose arrogance and egotism is so profound that they believe their ability to decide the lives and fates of others is a law of nature, absolutely entitling them to the largest share of society's goods. Never underestimate the lengths to which entrenched privilege and concentrated power will go to preserve the status quo and maintain absolute control. JFK, the Iraq War, and Guantanamo are signposts along that route.

In his acclaimed novel, *Cloud Atlas*, David Mitchell depicts the ultimate consumer society in which a crumbling civilization has lost control of its advanced technology; a brutally stratified world of technocrats and enforcers, consumers and genomically designed slaves call fabricants, a world tyrannically governed by a shadowy class of overlords, the "Juche." The protagonist, a female fabricant named Sonmi-451, tells the Unanimity Archivist the reality she has discovered in a passage that comprehends Ferguson, the War on Terror, and the very time in which we live:

> ...ignorance of the Other engenders fear; fear engenders hatred; hatred engenders violence; violence engenders further violence until the only "rights," the only law, are whatever is willed by the most powerful. In corpocracy, this means the Juche. What is willed by the Juche is the tidy extermination of a fabricant underclass.

So effective is the society's brainwashing, so isolated and compartmentalized the various social and professional classes, that the poor Archivist appointed to record the life of the revolutionary fabricant cannot believe the extent of the corruption she reveals (which includes recycling fabricants as food). Like all naïve patriots, the Archivist is led by his fear that Union revolution would bring an even worse tyranny; and he offers the argument Dixiecrats made against the Civil Rights Act of 1964, orthodoxy's timeless charge against the new and unfamiliar, in defense of the status quo:

> *Surely a program of incremental reform, of cautious steps, is the wisest way to proceed?*

Though "incremental reform" and "cautious steps" are precisely what ExxonMobil, Monsanto and Dow are counting on, we cannot afford such a program where global warming, energy policy and the future of human society is concerned.

To cite Dr. Henry Goose's memorable apophthegm from *Cloud Atlas*: "The weak are meat the strong do eat."

We shall almost certainly need to redesign capital and currency or else replace them with universal credit from which the profit motive has been detached. To achieve the peaceful redistribution of resources and services, to eliminate poverty and the "taste" for war, we will have to make universal credit available to every person on the planet.

Failure to embrace needed change is permanent surrender to Austerity at a Graveyard. The graveyard is, of course, capitalism.

 **Dennis Weiser** earned his Liberal Arts B.A. at Westminster College of Missouri in 1978 and his Master of Arts in Philosophy at The University of Kansas in 1991. He has worked as a deckhand on the Mississippi, curator at an art gallery, taught middle school science and college philosophy. He is former weekly columnist for The Kansas City Business Journal and book reviewer for NPR affiliate KCUR-FM in Kansas City, Missouri, where he has lived since 1981. In June 2015, October Surprise and 3RD AWAKENING BOOKS will publish *Sinister Dynamic*, Volume Three (*The Challenge: Redefining Work, Equality & Authority*). A member of the Academy of American Poets, Dennis is currently writing his third novel, a historical mystery set in 1879 Java against the backdrop of Dutch Colonial exploitation.

www.ingramcontent.com/pod-product-compliance
Lightning Source LLC
Chambersburg PA
CBHW021904170526
45157CB00005B/1962